Welland Ontario Book 1 in Colour Photos, Saving Our History One Photo at a Time

Photography
by Barbara Raué
2016

Series Name:
Cruising Ontario

Book 138: Welland Book 1

Cover photo: 131 Aqueduct Street, Page 8

Series Name: Cruising Ontario
Saving Our History One Photo at a Time
in colour photos

Books Available in Alphabetical Order:
Aberfoyle, Acton, Alton, Ancaster, Arthur, Aylmer, Ayr, Bloomingdale, Brantford, Burlington, Caledon, Caledonia, Cambridge, Clifford, Conestogo, Delhi, Dorchester to Aylmer, Drayton, Drumbo, Dundas, Eden Mills, Elmira, Elora, Fergus, Guelph, Hagersville, Hamilton, Hanover, Harriston, Hespeler, Jarvis, Kitchener, Linwood, Listowel, London, Lucknow, Mono, Mount Forest, Neustadt, New Hamburg, Niagara-on-the-Lake, Oakville, Orangeville, Orillia, Owen Sound, Palmerston, Peterborough, Port Elgin, Preston, Rockwood, Seaforth, Sheffield, Shelburne, Simcoe, Southampton, St. Jacobs, St. Thomas, Stoney Creek, Stratford, Tillsonburg, Waterdown, Waterford, Waterloo, Wellesley, Wingham

Book 114-116: Waterloo
Book 117-119: Windsor
Book 120: Amherstburg
Book 122: Essex
Book 123-124: Kingsville
Book 125-127: Woodstock
Book 128: Thamesford
Book 129: St. Mary's
Book 133-136: Sarnia
Book 137: Petrolia
Book 138-139: Welland

Other Books by Barbara Raue

Coins of Gold

Arrows, Indians and Love

The Life and Times of Barbara
Volume 1: Inventions That Have Enhanced My Life
Volume 2: Entertainment That I Have Enjoyed
Volume 3: East Coast Trips
Volume 4: Olympics Have Always Intrigued Me
Volume 5: Wonders of the World
Volume 6: Caribbean Cruises We Have Enjoyed
Volume 7: Animals
Volume 8: Storms and Other Major Disasters in My Lifetime
Volume 9: Wars, Terrorist Attacks and Major Disasters

The Cromwell Family Book

Laura Secord Discovered

Daddy Where Are You?

Visit Barbara's website to view all of her books
http://barbararaue.ca

Table of Contents

Welland is located in the centre of Niagara. Within a half-hour, residents can travel to Niagara Falls, Niagara-on-the-Lake, St. Catharines, Port Colborne or Buffalo. It has been traditionally known as the place *where rails and water meet*, referring to the railways from Buffalo to Toronto and Southwestern Ontario, and the waterways of the Welland Canal and Welland River, which played a great role in the city's development. The city is separated by the Welland River and Welland Canal which links Lake Erie and Lake Ontario.

The city was first settled in 1788 by United Empire Loyalists.

Welland, because of its proximity to the Sir Adam Beck hydroelectric station at Niagara Falls, was historically known for its steel, automotive, and textile industries. Manufacturing firms were the biggest employers in Welland, with companies like Union Carbide, United Steel, Plymouth Cordage Company, three drop forges, a cotton mill, and the Atlas Steel Company, as well as general manufacturing plants, influencing the shaping of early Welland.

The Plymouth Cordage Company was the first major industrial company to open a plant in Welland in 1906. It was a rope making company with headquarters in Plymouth, Massachusetts; it became the largest manufacturer of rope and twine in the world. Plymouth binder twine was popular among farmers to package farm crops such as grass, wheat and straw, and was the inspiration for the naming of the Plymouth brand of automobiles first produced in 1928. Many workers who relocated to Welland from the company's operations in Plymouth were of Italian origin. To minimise the potential effects of cultural and language barriers, Plymouth Cordage sent four foremen to Welland: one was Italian, one was French, one was German and one was English.

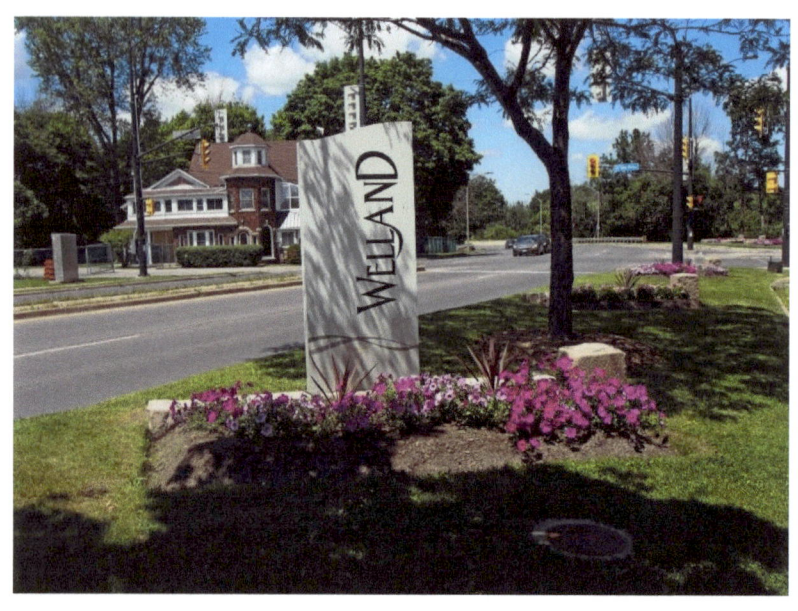

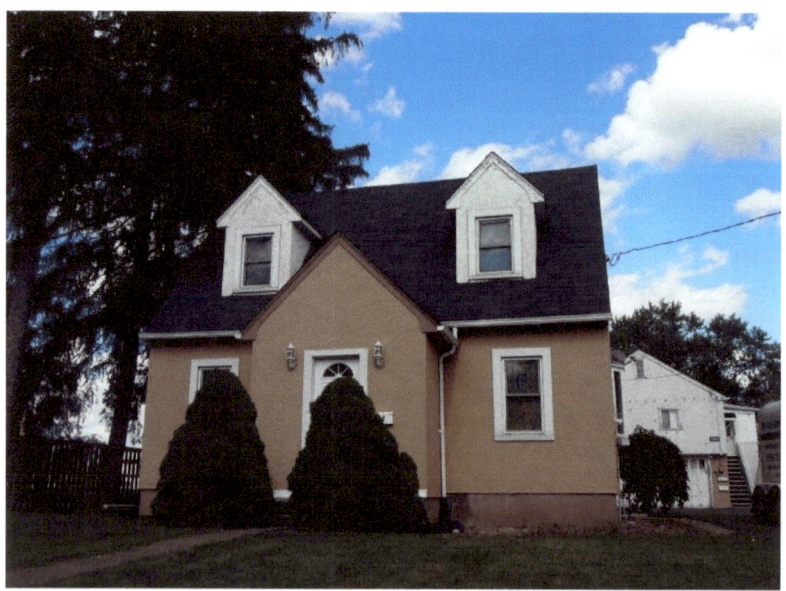

152 Aqueduct Street – Gothic, dormers

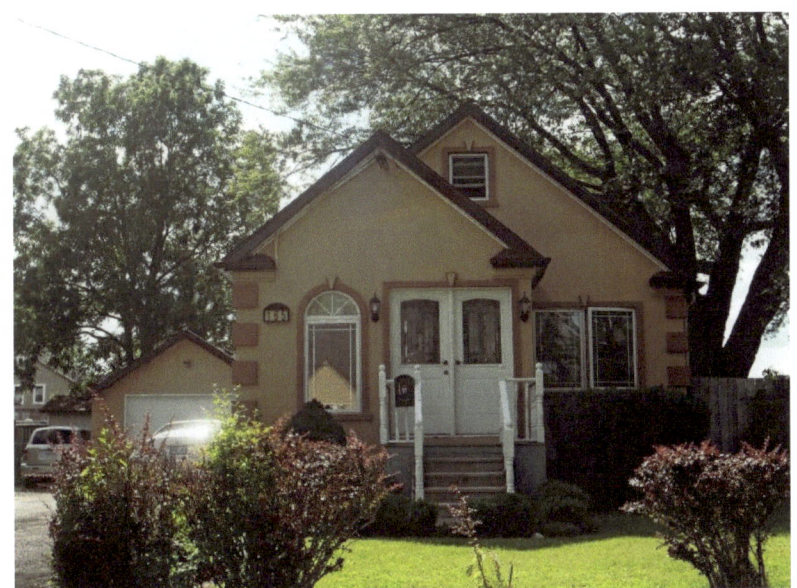

165 Aqueduct Street – vernacular – cornice return on gables

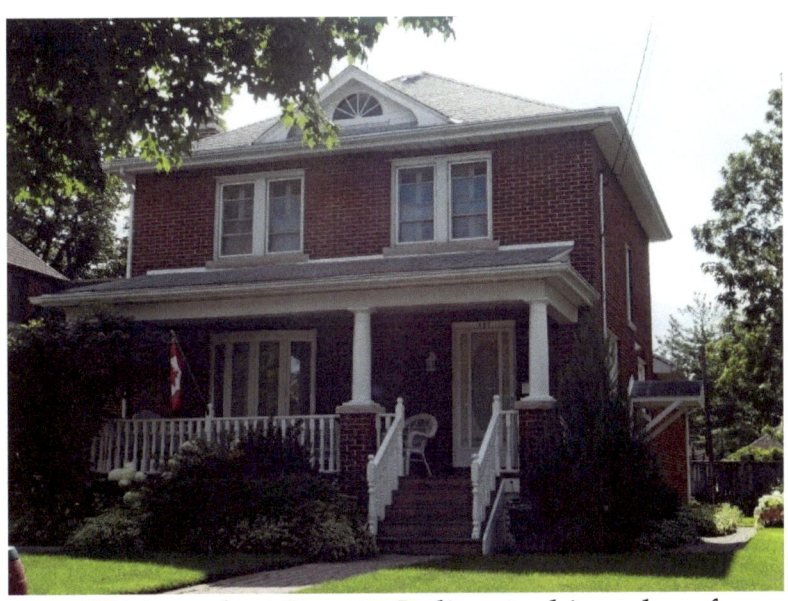

157 Aqueduct Street – Italianate, hipped roof

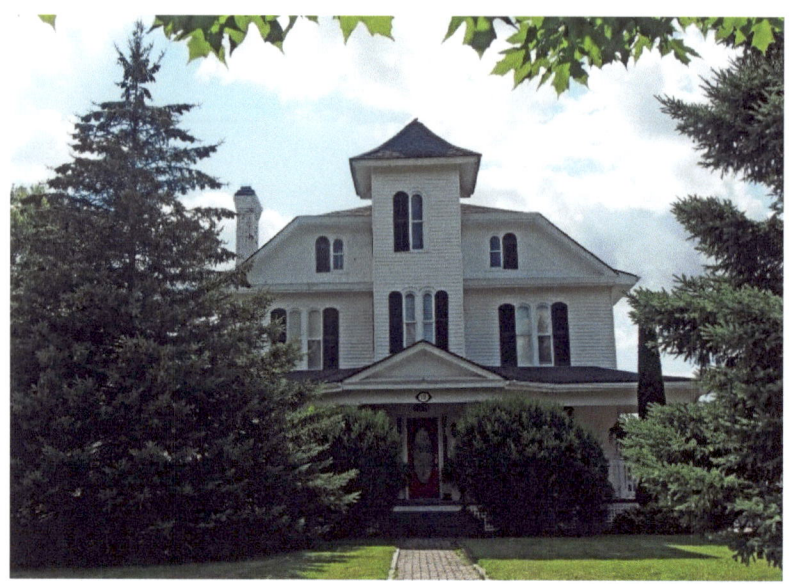

131 Aqueduct Street – Bagar-Bison House – 1880 - Victorian
Two-storey tower, pediment, fish scale pattern on upper
storey, sidelights around door

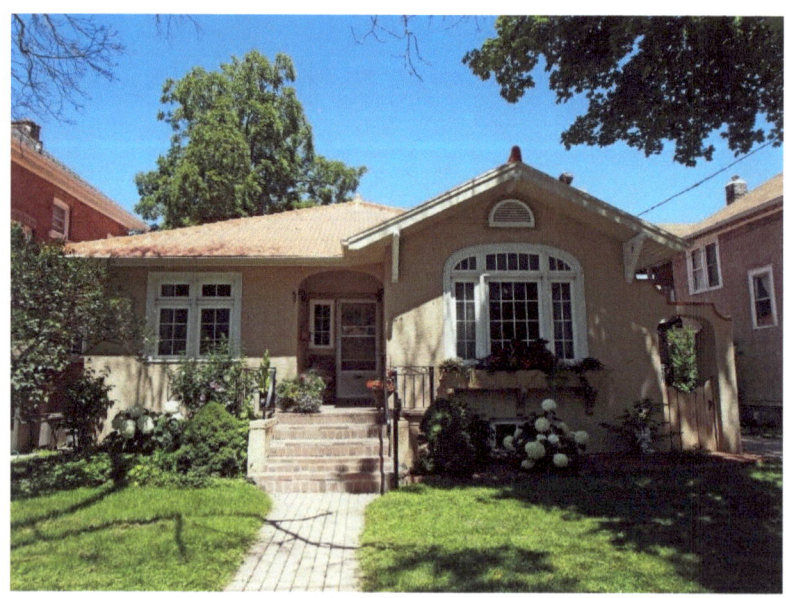

104 Bald Street

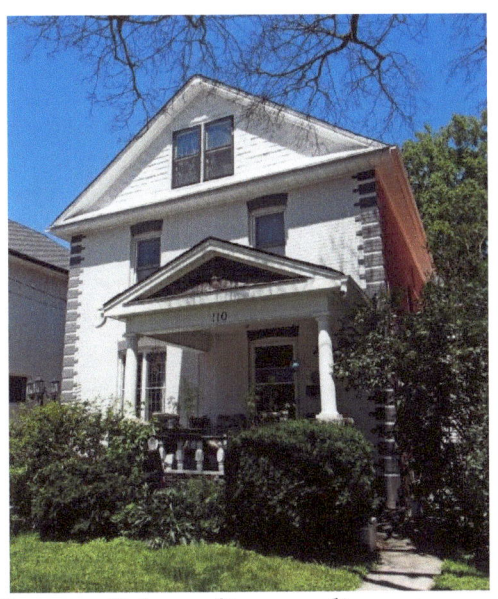

110 Bald Street – Edwardian, pediment, corner quoins

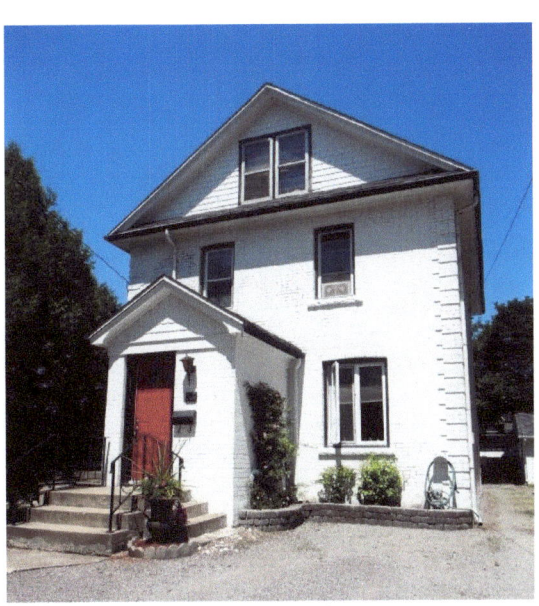

Bald Street – Edwardian, pediment, corner quoins

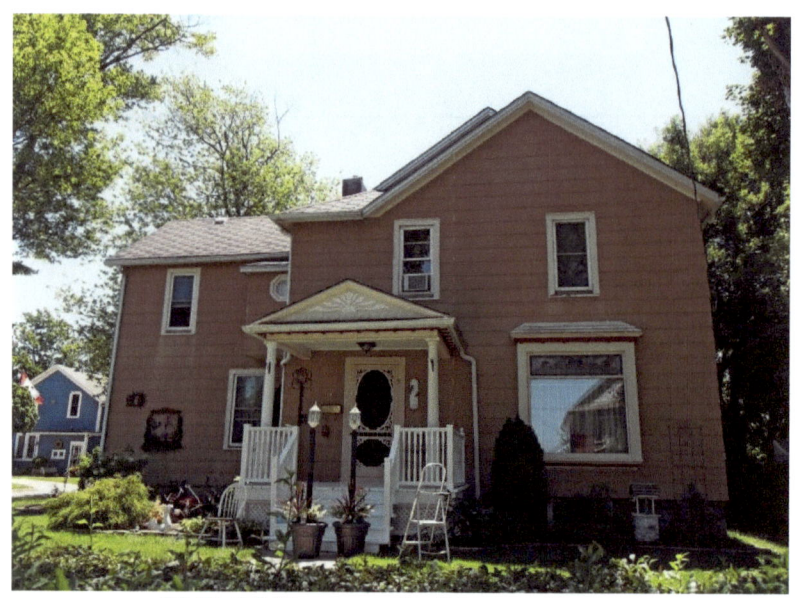

93 Bald Street – Gothic, pediment

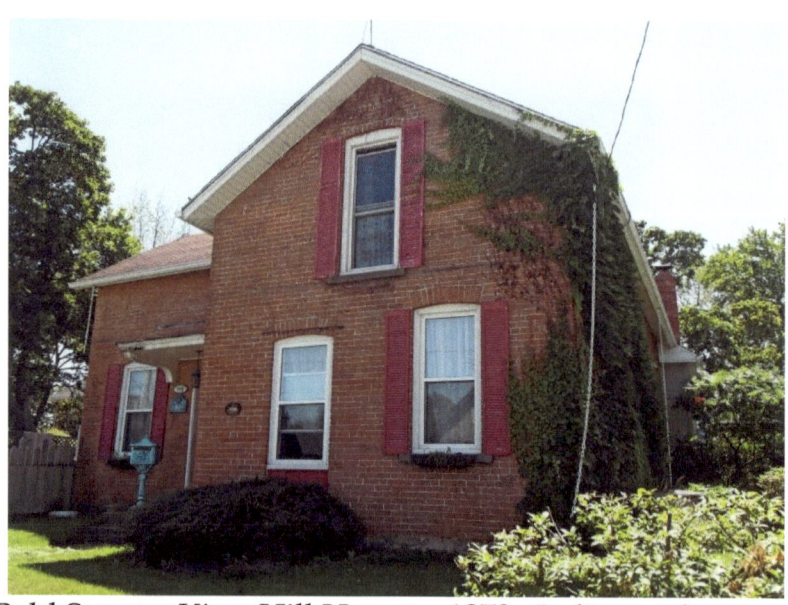

81 Bald Street – King-Hill House – 1872 –Italianate house with arched openings and first floor bay window

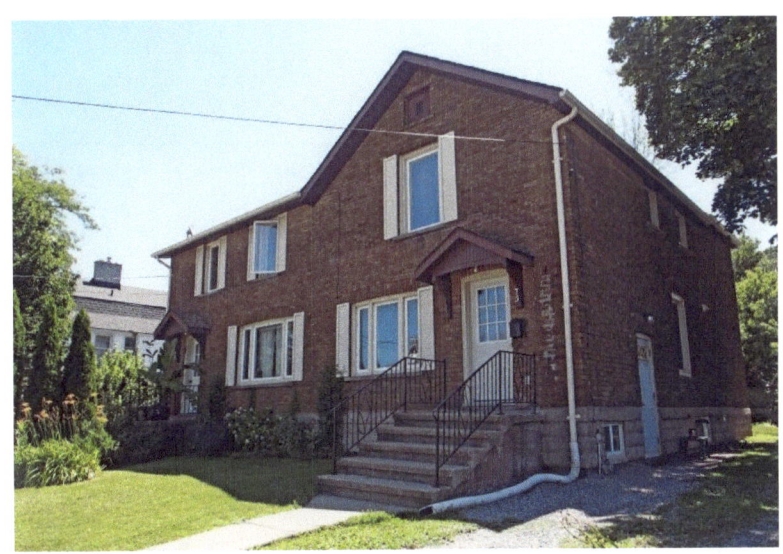

75 Bald Street - Gothic

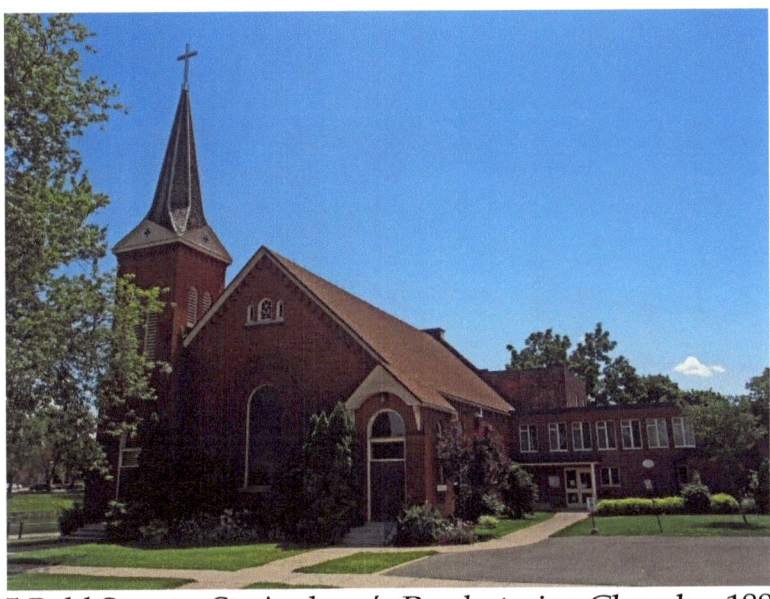

25 Bald Street – St. Andrew's Presbyterian Church – 1889
Red brick, single-storey church – Norman (Romanesque) and
Italianate characteristics – tall octagonal "broach" spire, semi-
circular arched windows

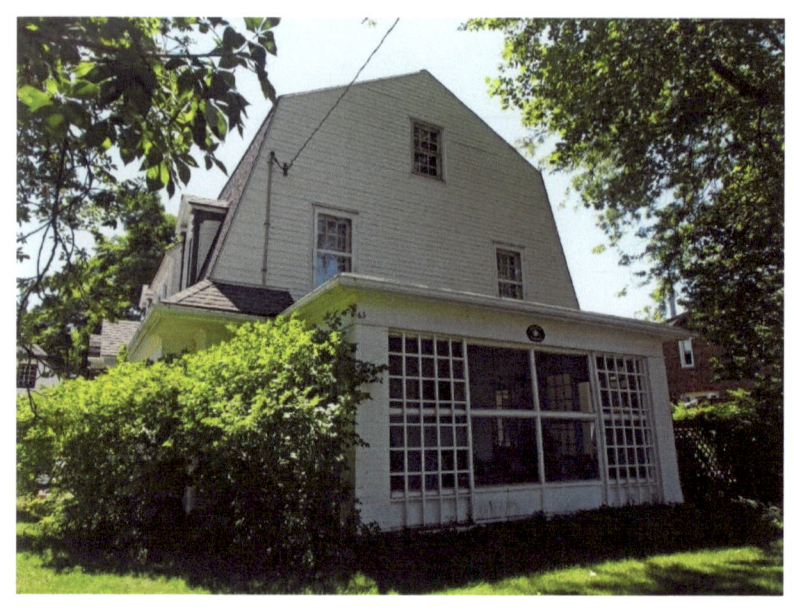

65 Bald Street – gambrel roof

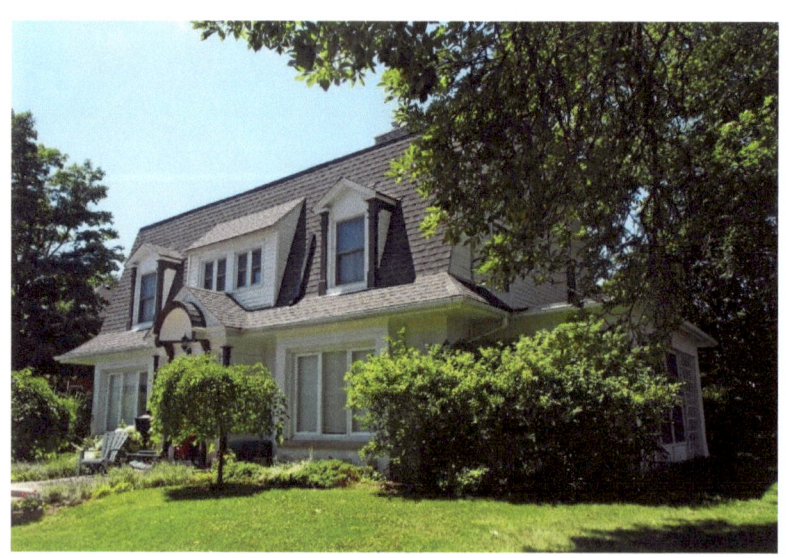

Dormers

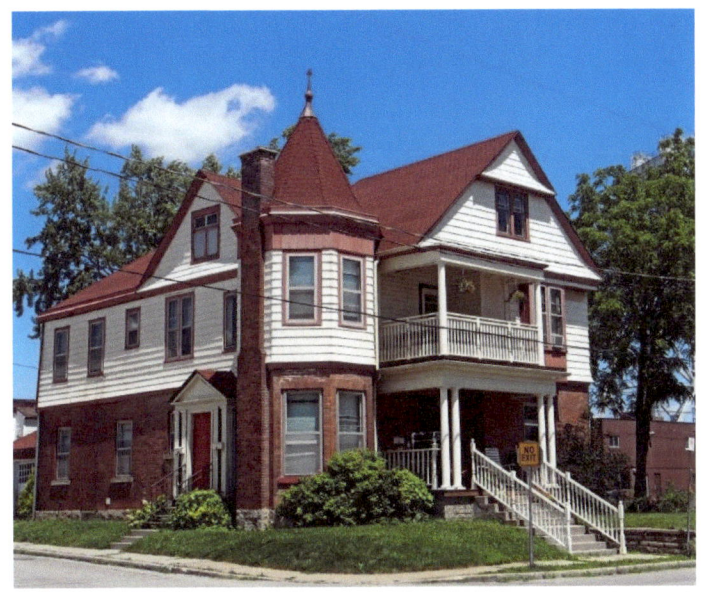

30 Bald Street – Queen Anne style, two-storey turret with cone-shaped cap, second floor sleeping porch

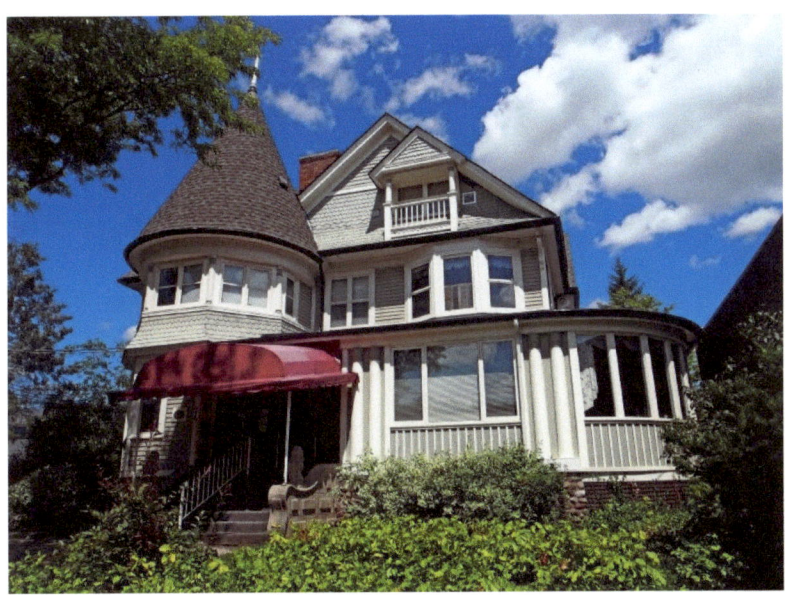

24 Burgar Street – The Glasgow-Fortner House – 1859 – Queen Anne style – now Rinderlins Dining Rooms

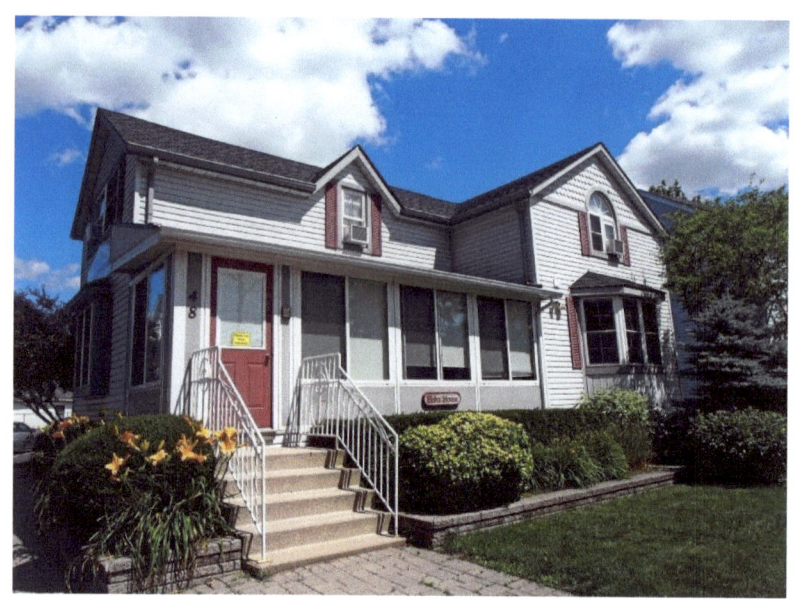

48 Burgar Street – Gothic – fish scale pattern in large gable
Elisha House

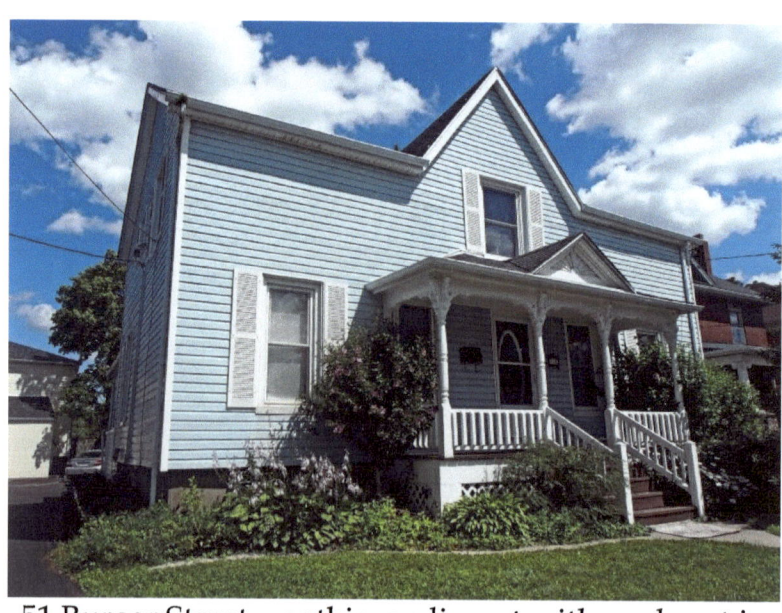

51 Burgar Street – gothic, pediment with sunburst in
tympanum, bric-a-brac on verandah

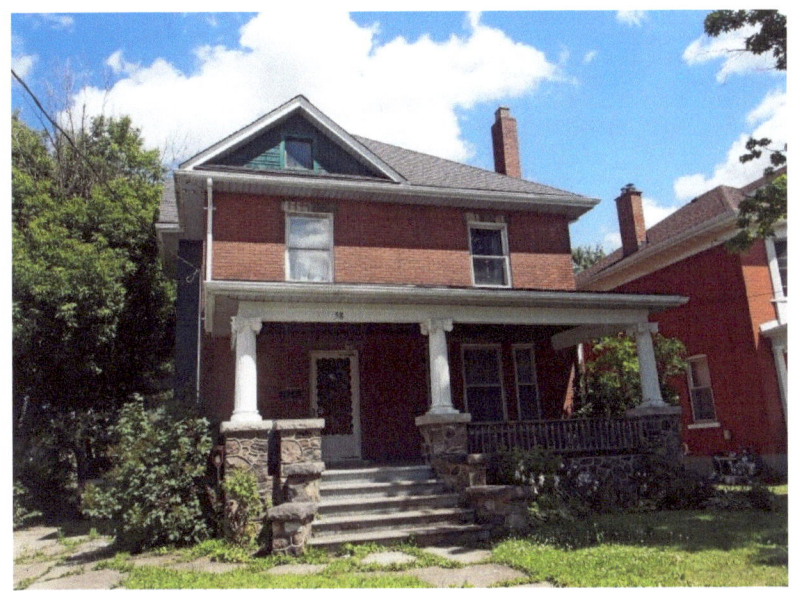

58 Burgar Street – Italianate – hipped roof, Ionic capitals on verandah pillars

Catherine Street

The Paving of Welland's Street

The brick road on Catherine Street was completed in December 1913. It is a visual reminder of the early 1900s, an important period of rapid change and industrialization in Welland's history. Constructed of medium red "Metropolitan" paving brick manufactured in Michigan, it was laid in a stretcher bond pattern over a six-inch concrete base

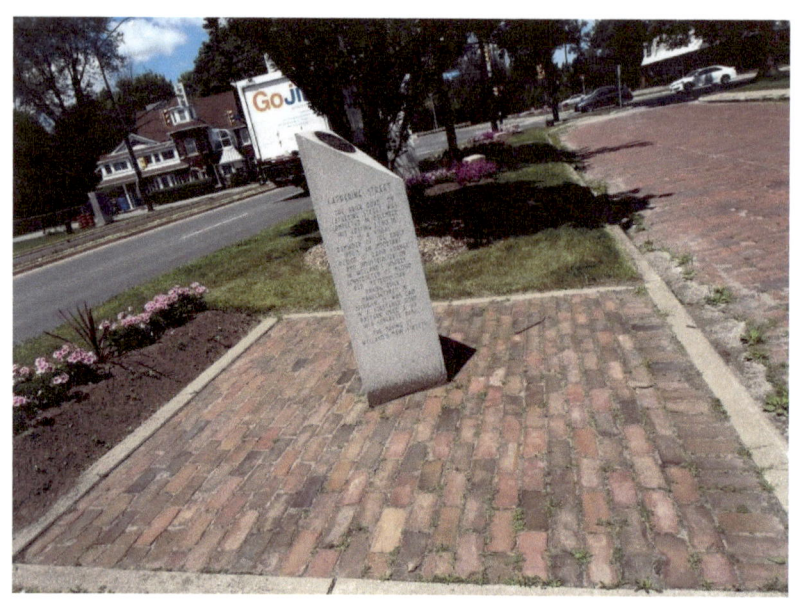

Catherine Street

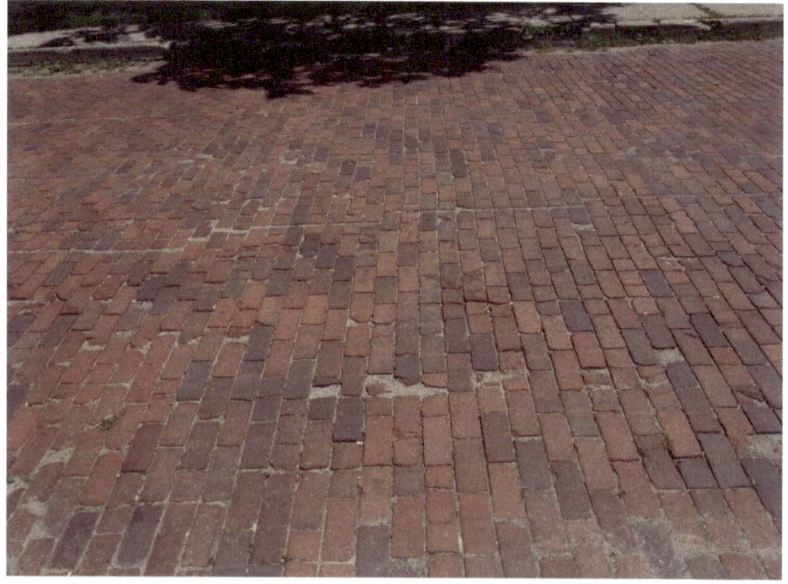

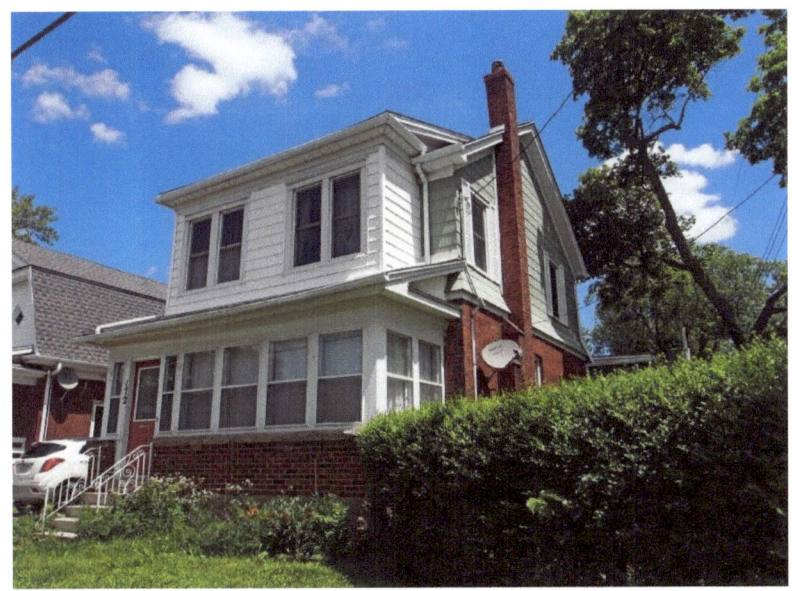

172 Dennistoun Street

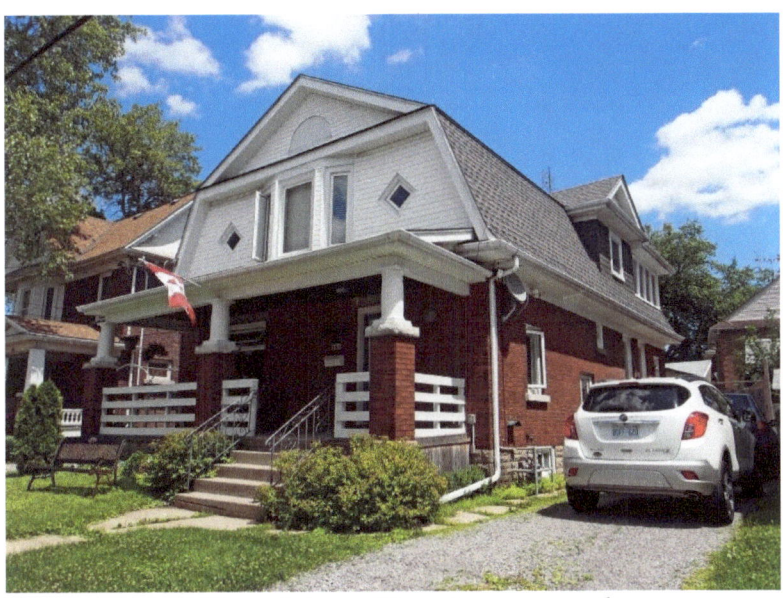

168 Dennistoun Street - vernacular

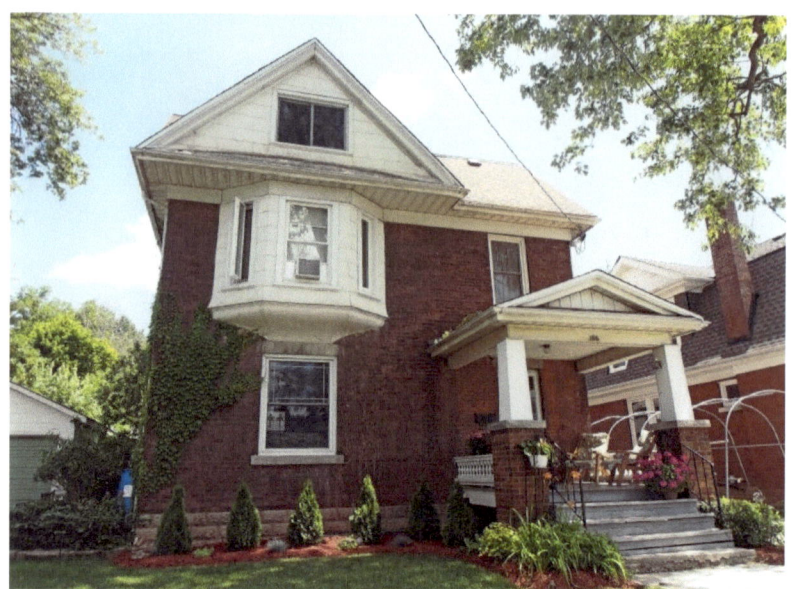

166 Dennistoun Street – Edwardian, oriel window, pediment

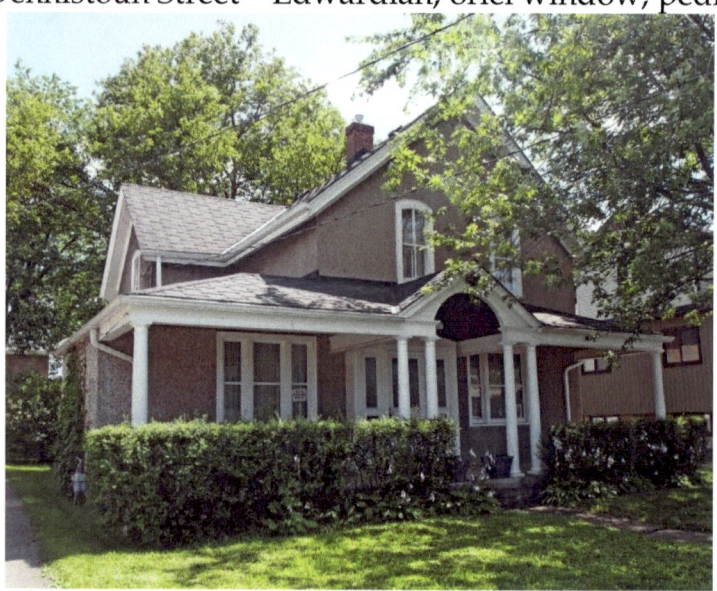

179 Division Street – Lowe-Arthurs House – 1878 - Victorian Italianate style – front porch with entrance framed by a Palladian arch spanning two columns, two over two arched windows, panelled doors have china knobs

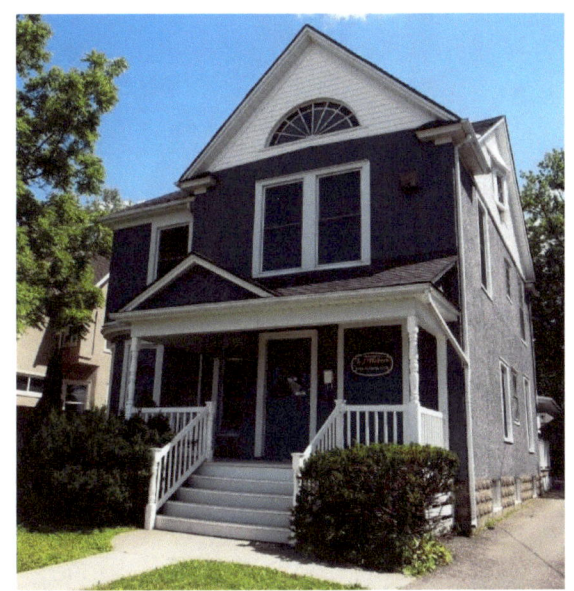

187 Division Street – Edwardian, pediment

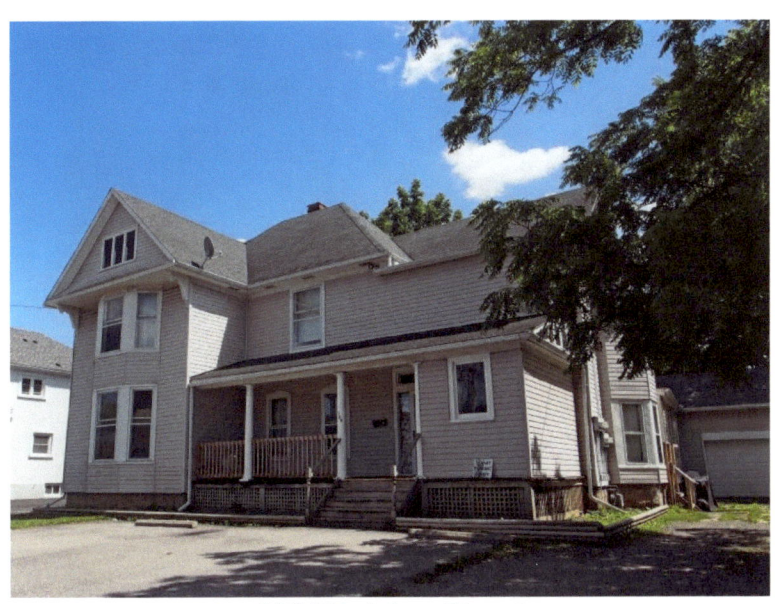

199 Division Street

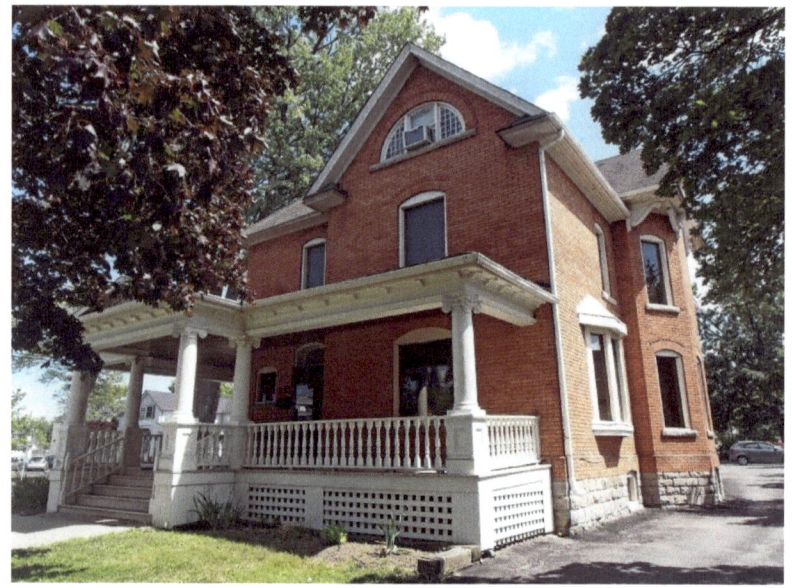

233 Division Street – Grantham-Bovine House – Victorian style, coffered eaves, arched window with decorative terra-cotta hood moulding

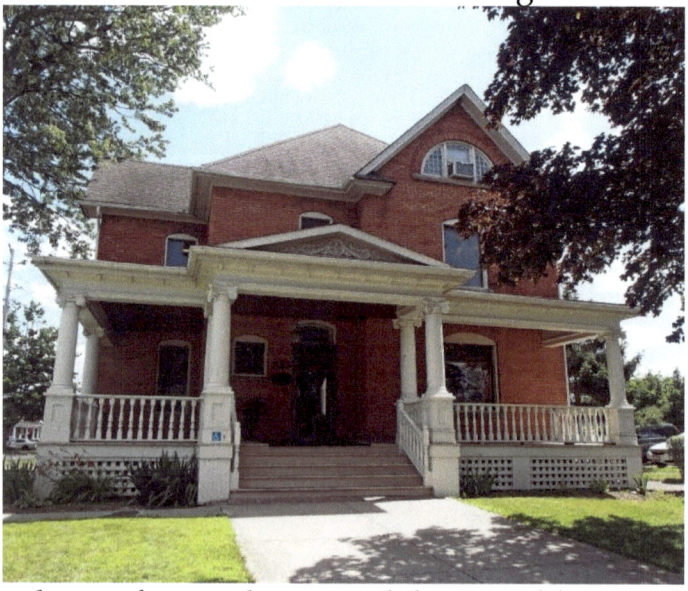

Ionic columns for porch, egg and dart moulding, pediment with decorated tympanum

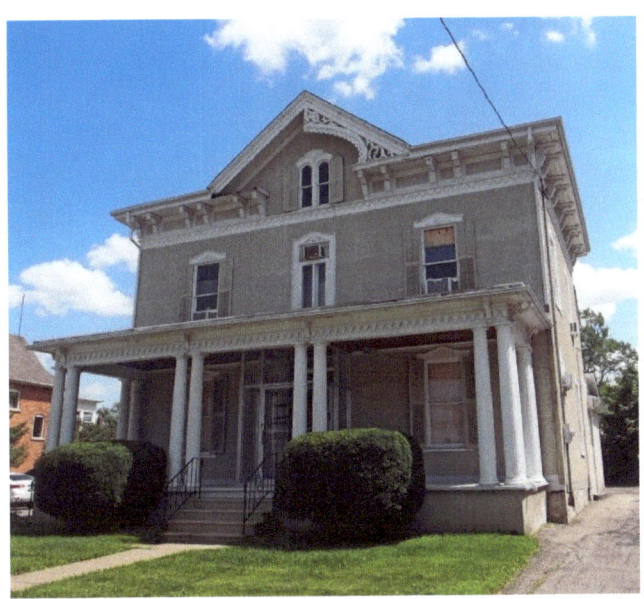

221 Division Street – McCollum-Harcourt House – late 1870s
2½ storey stuccoed house, Italianate style – open verandah
supported by wooden columns, double eave brackets, lacy
verge board under central peak above a double semi-circular
window

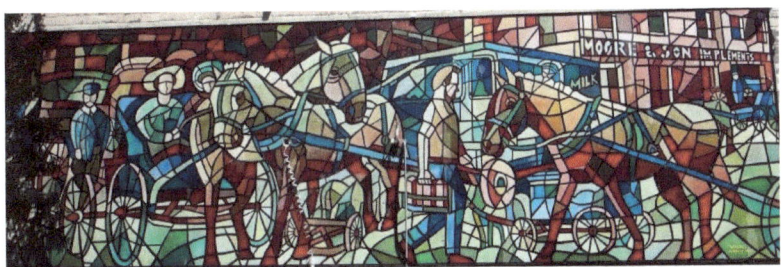

Wagons mural – 266 Division Street – by Barrie artist Andrew
Miles – stained glass effect of a variety of turn-of-the-century
wagons and buggies depicts the important part played by
horse-drawn vehicles in Welland's history.

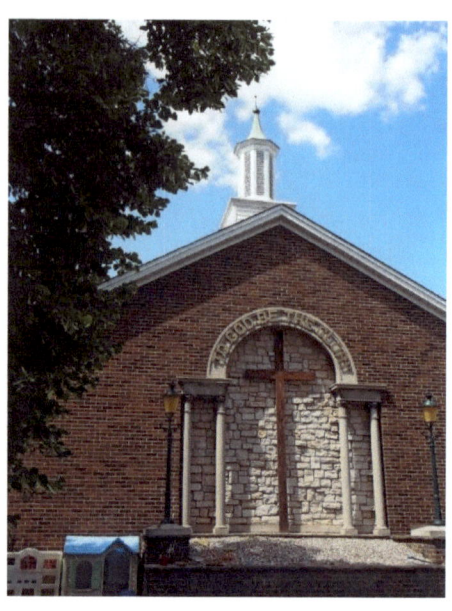

224 Division Street – Christ Community Church

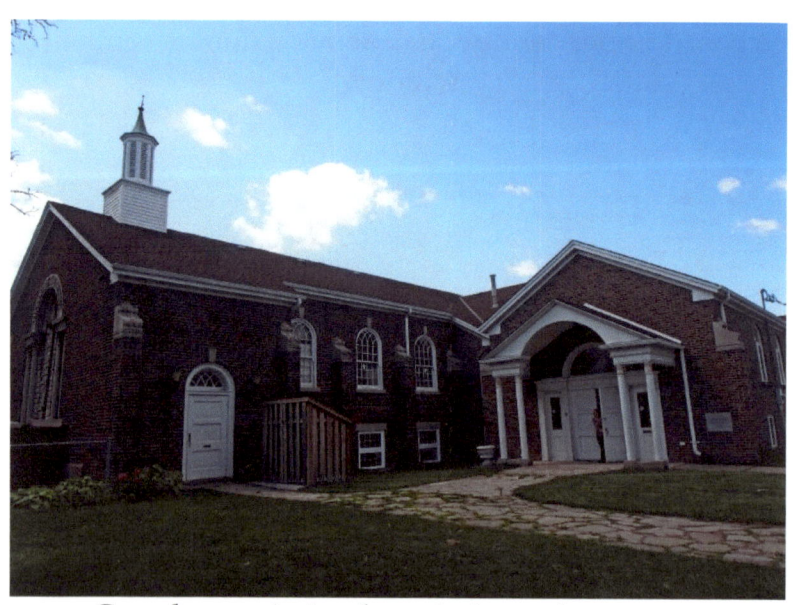

Cupola, semi-circular windows, buttresses

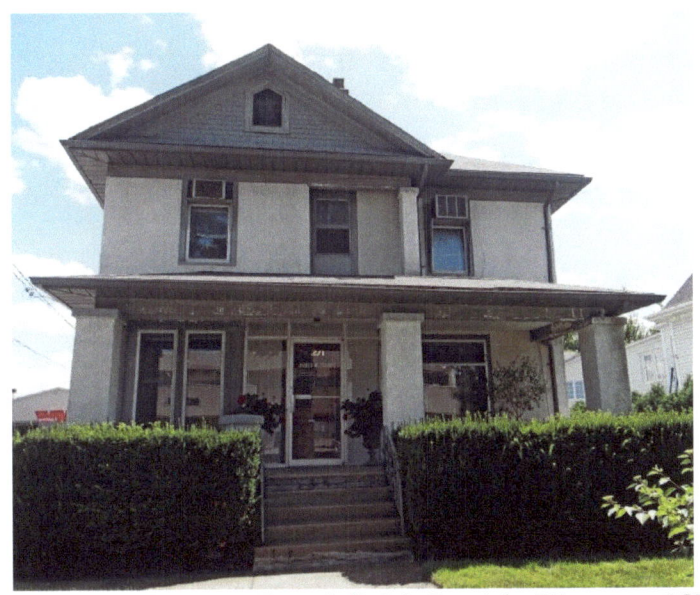

271 Division Street – Brookfield-Cupido House – 1875 –
Edwardian Classical/Queen Anne style – square columned
front porch, large plate glass window with stained glass
above, fish scale shingles, stylized Gothic window under gable

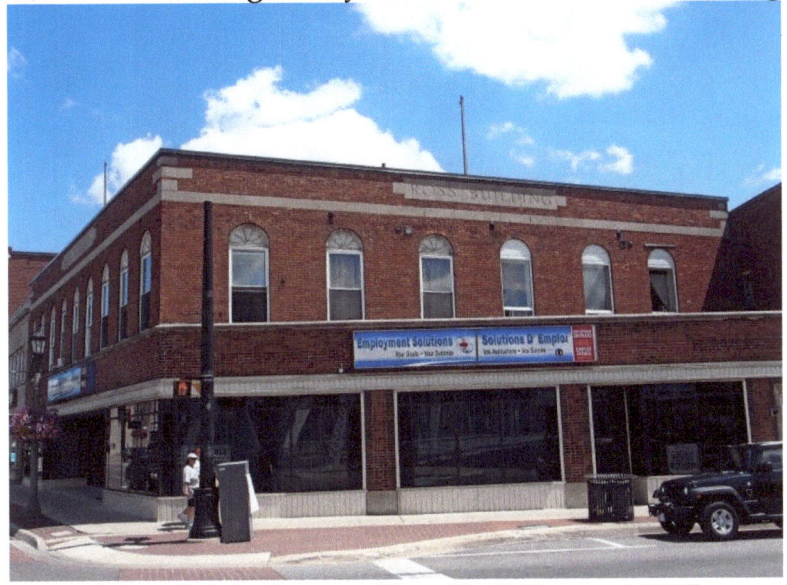

3 East Main Street – Ross Building – c. 1873

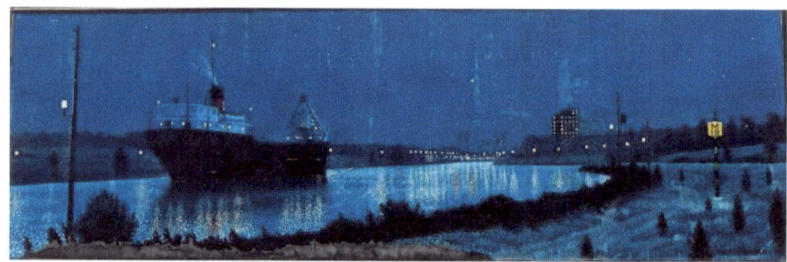

"Upbound at Midnight" – 228 East Main Street - painted by local artist Ross Beard - night scene features lights reflecting softly on the water as a ship named the Erindale proceeds south to Port Colborne along the magnificent Welland Canal

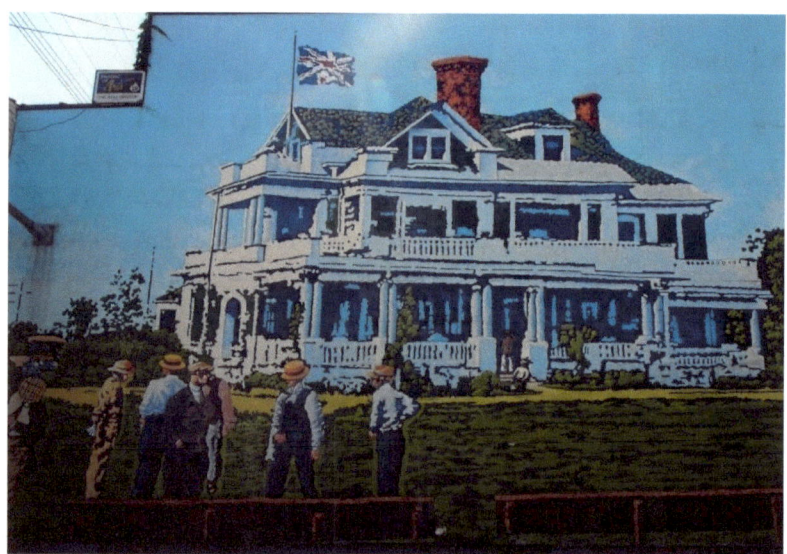

The Welland Club mural – corner of Hellems Avenue and East Main Street – The exclusive Welland Club situated on the banks of the canal on King Street is depicted in all its glory in the 1920s or 1930s. Toronto artist John Hood captures the period with the blazing Union Jack and the lawn bowlers in the foreground. The structure burned to the ground in 2011.

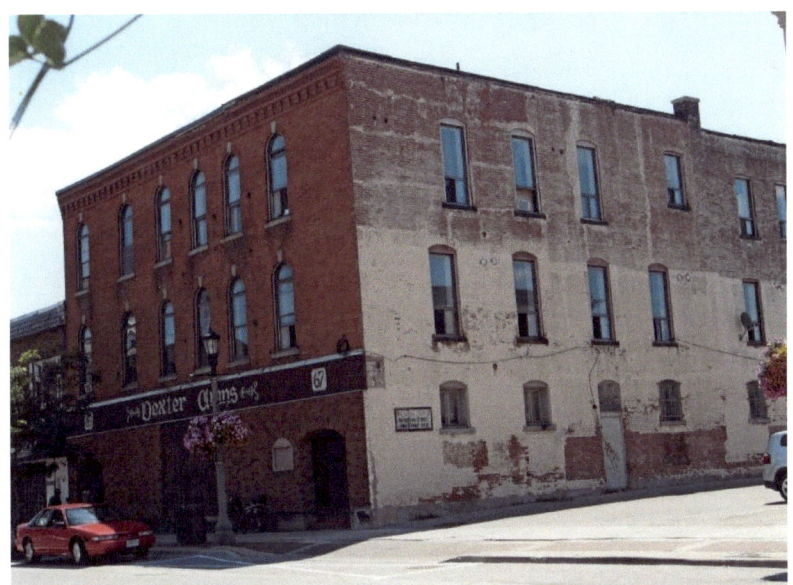

67-69 East Main Street – Dexter House – 1873 - three-storey brick, Italianate

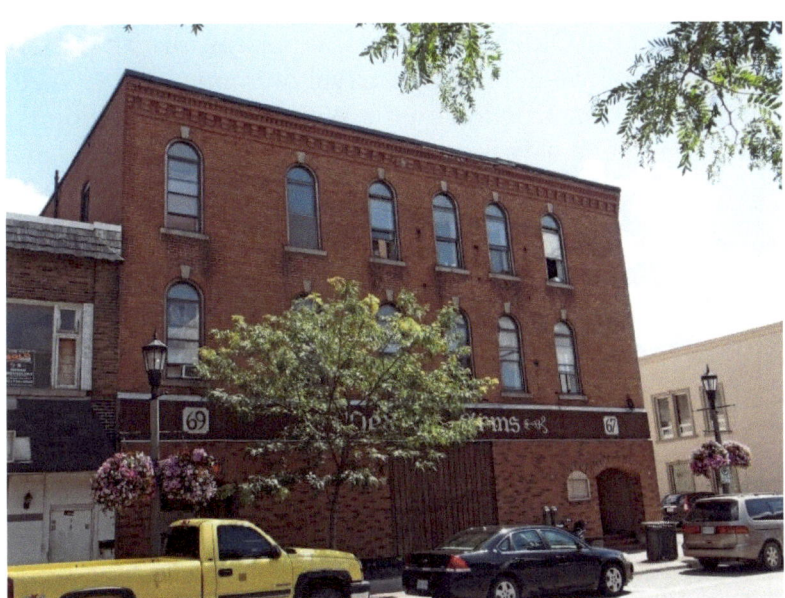

Shape and awkward spacing of the windows make the front of this structure unique

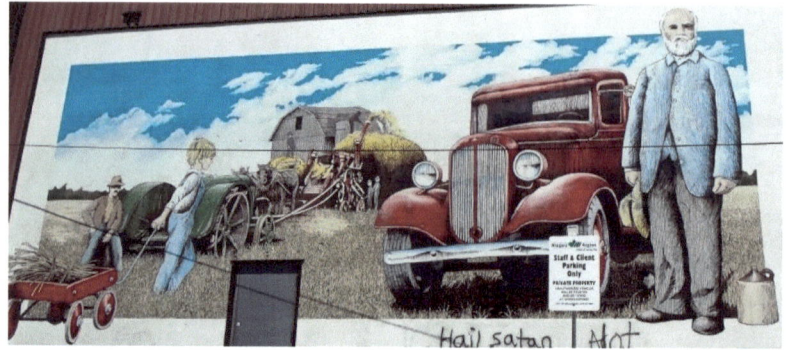

"Little Helper" – family comradery formed on the farm

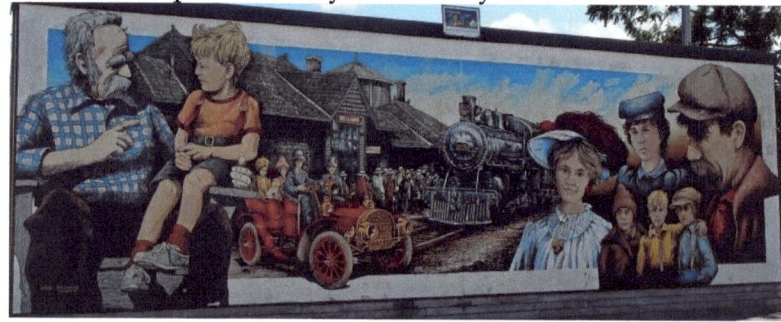

"Tell Me About the Olden Days" by Chemainus, British Columbia artist Dan Sawatzky – depicts the arrival of immigrants to Welland circa 1910. Construction on the Welland Canal provided employment, while new industries offered permanent jobs and a reason to settle down.

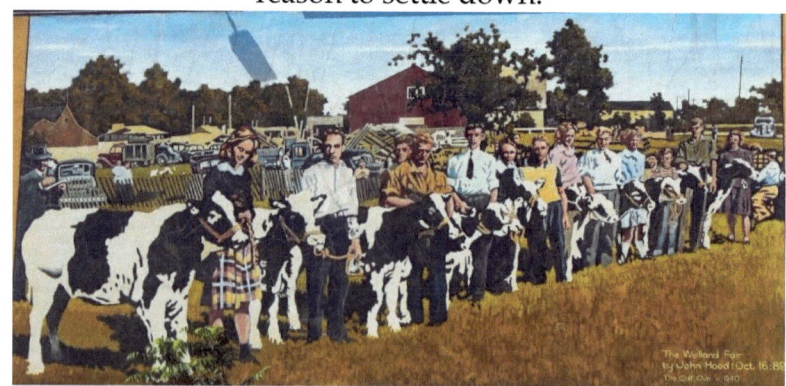

Welland Fair, 228 East Main Street by Toronto artist John Hood – this image and the next two – the 4H Club shows off livestock winners circa 1940 – The Calf Club

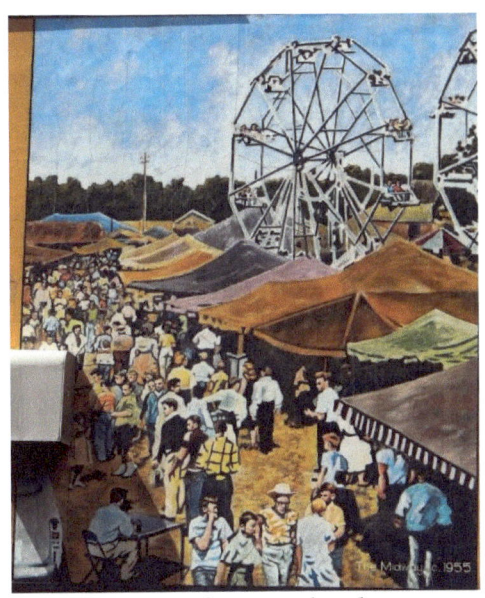

The Midway c. 1955 – the ferris wheel acts as a focus of the three images

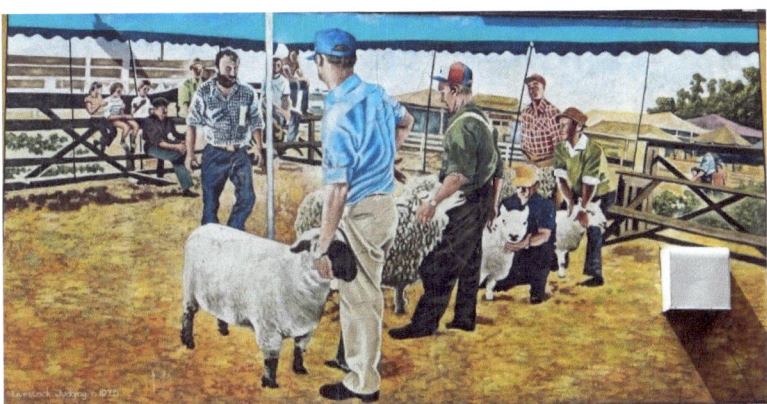

The Welland Fair – by John Hood – the livestock judge scrutinizes a line of sheep

The Cordage Community, 212 East Main Street by local artist
Marsha Charlebols

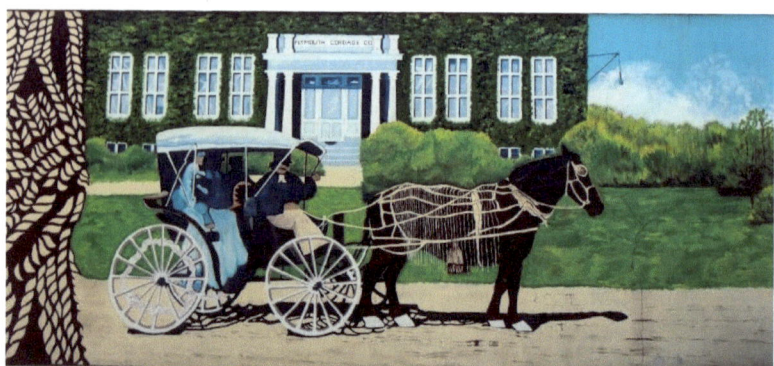

The history of one of Welland's first industries, the Plymouth
Cordage Company is depicted. The rope and binder twine
manufacturer opened for business in 1906. The "Cordage
People" believed in leisure activities as strongly as they did
their work, and were known for their fairs, games and family
gatherings. The ladies below are involved in a tug of war.

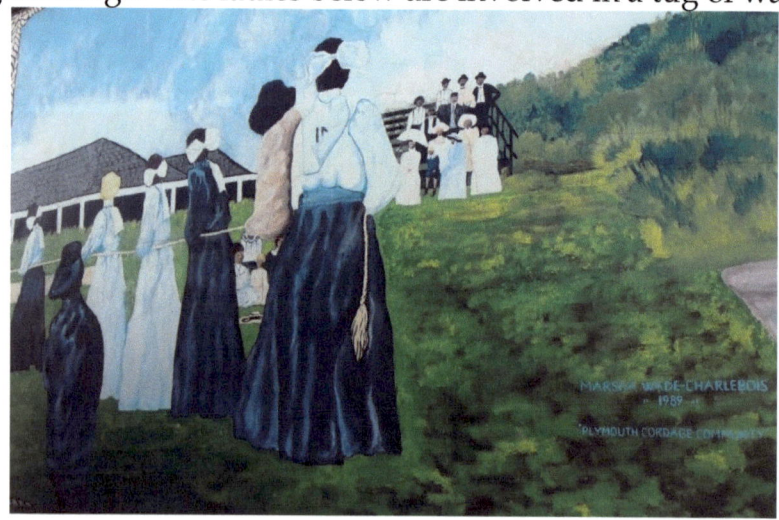

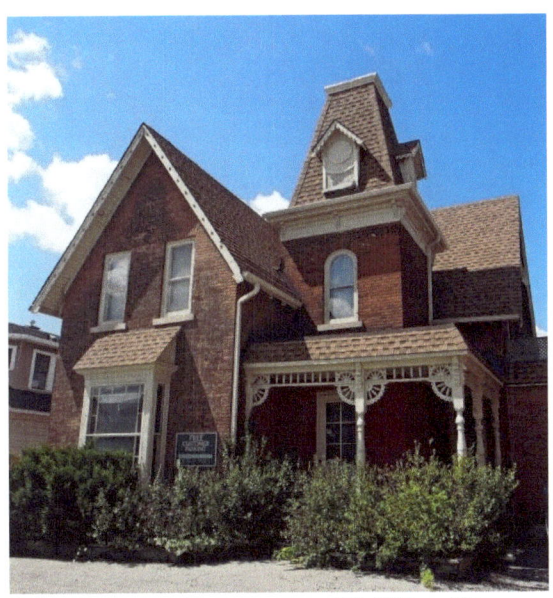

204 East Main Street – Lawrence-Phillips House – c. 1890 – Victorian style with a mixture of Gothic, Tuscan Italianate and Queen Anne elements

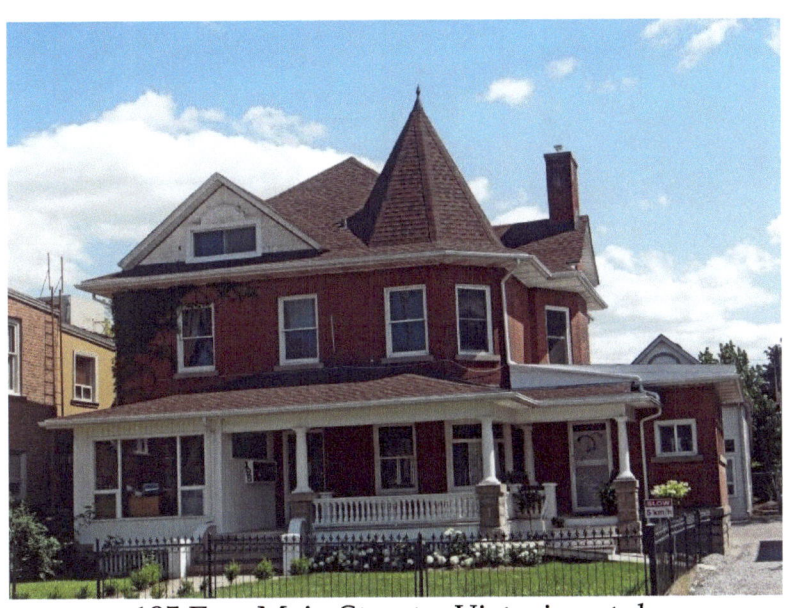

195 East Main Street – Victorian style

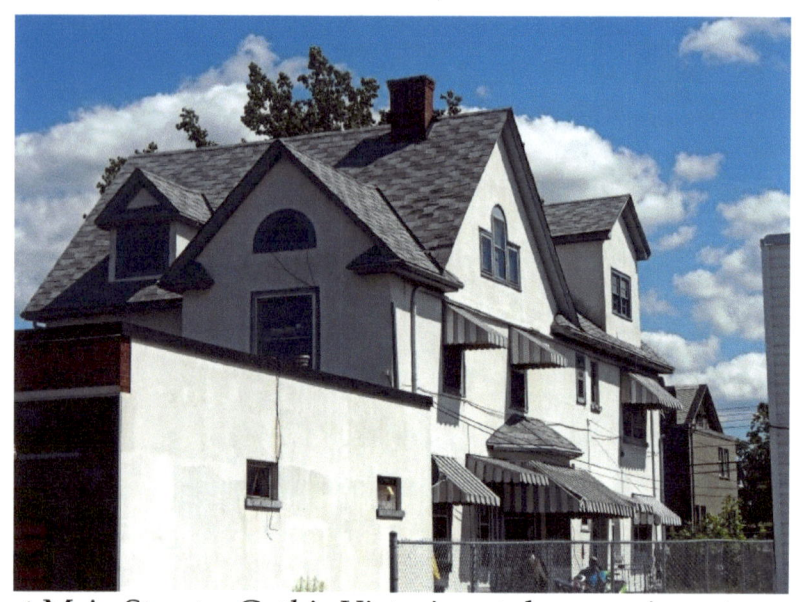

East Main Street – Gothic Victorian style – cornice return on gables, Palladian window

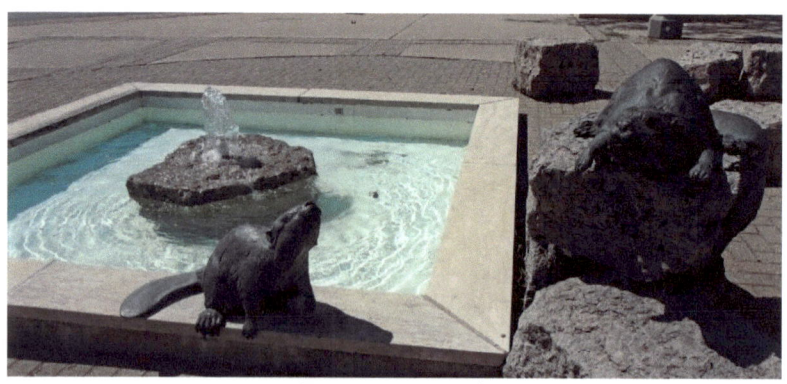

Beaver Pond

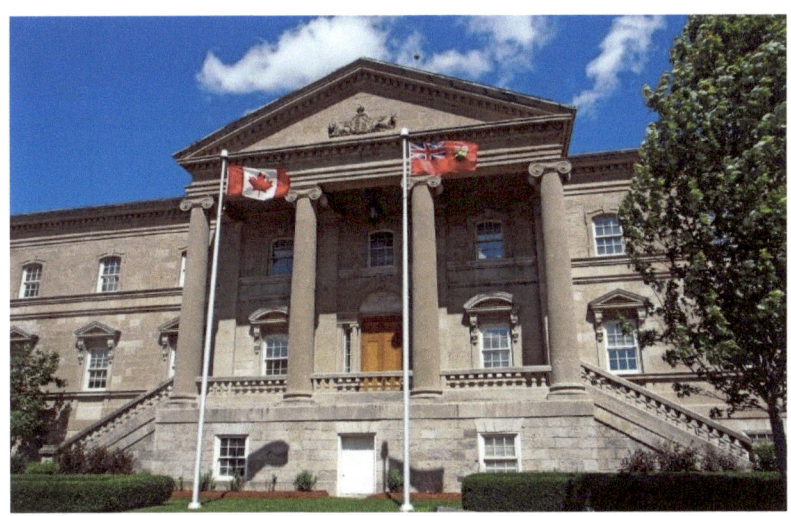

102 East Main Street - Welland County Court House – built in 1855-56, four years after the creation of Welland County; Neo-Classical style, built of Queenston limestone – the front of the building is dominated by a huge projecting portico surmounted by a classical pediment and four large Ionic columns, sidelights beside door

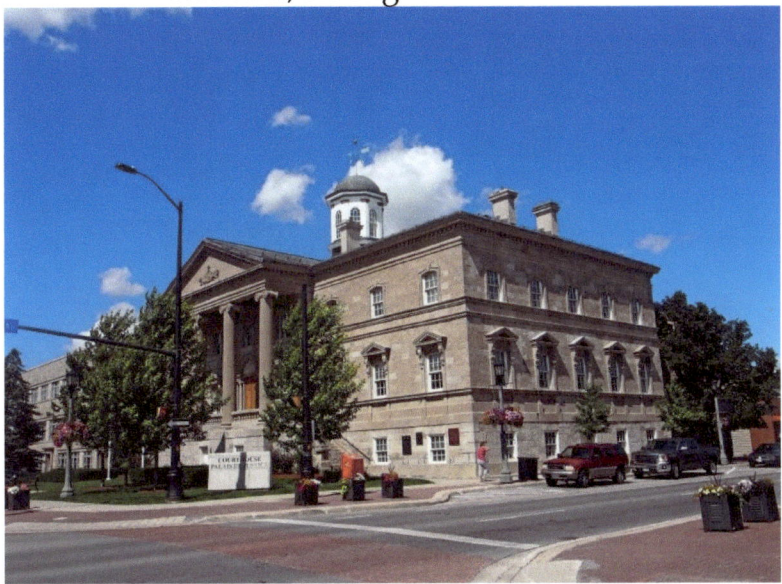

Walls are three to four feet thick, grand court room with central cupola for natural lighting

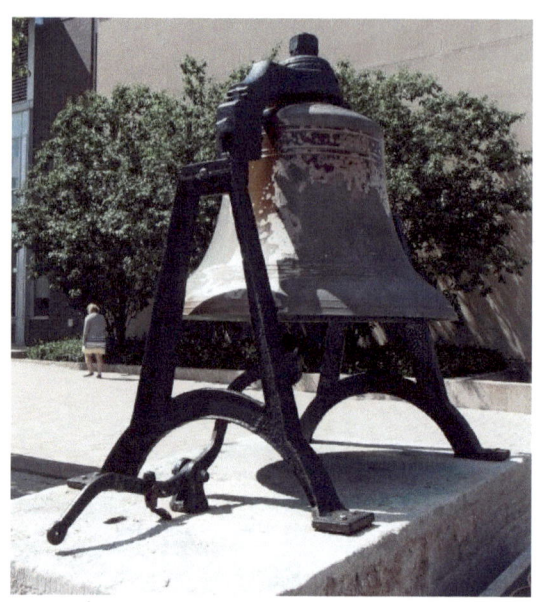

Following a fire in 1884 in the fire hall, this bell was commissioned to act as a civic fire alarm. The bell remained at the Cross Street Fire Hall until 1901 when it was moved to the new Town Hall at King and Division Streets.

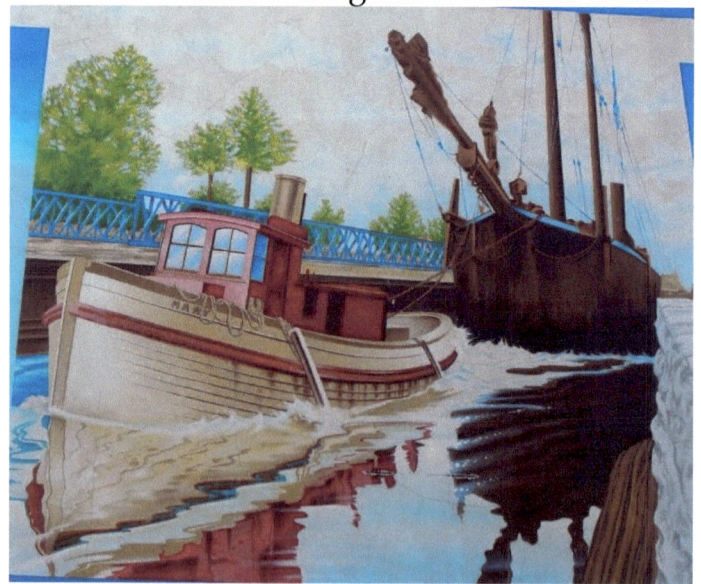

Mary tugboat

Tugboat mural – 77 East Main Street
– by Ottawa artist Stefan Bell

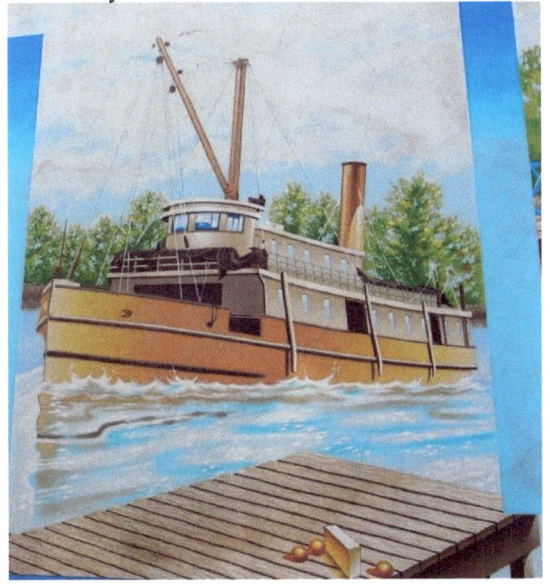

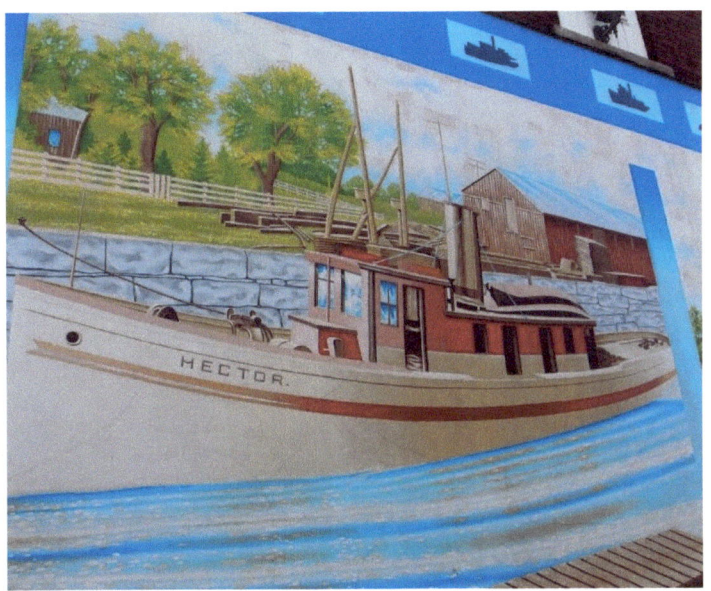

Hector tugboat – the tugboats pulled barges and ships
through the waterway – c. 1920s

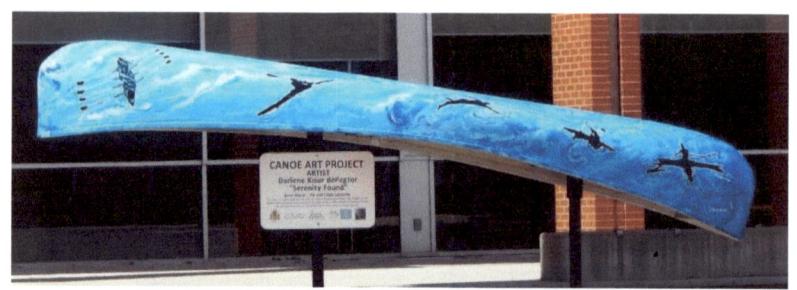

Canoe Art Project – "Serenity Found"
by artist Darlene Kisur dePagtor

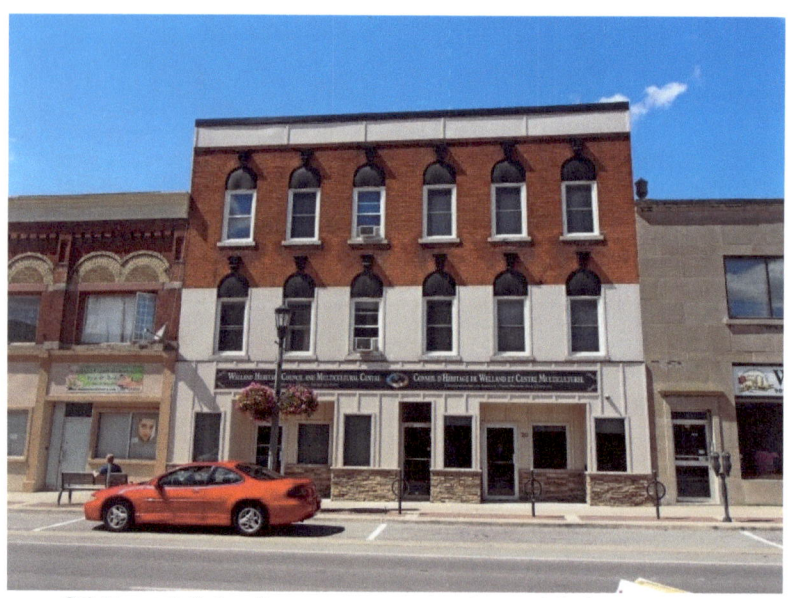

26 East Main Street – voussoirs with keystones

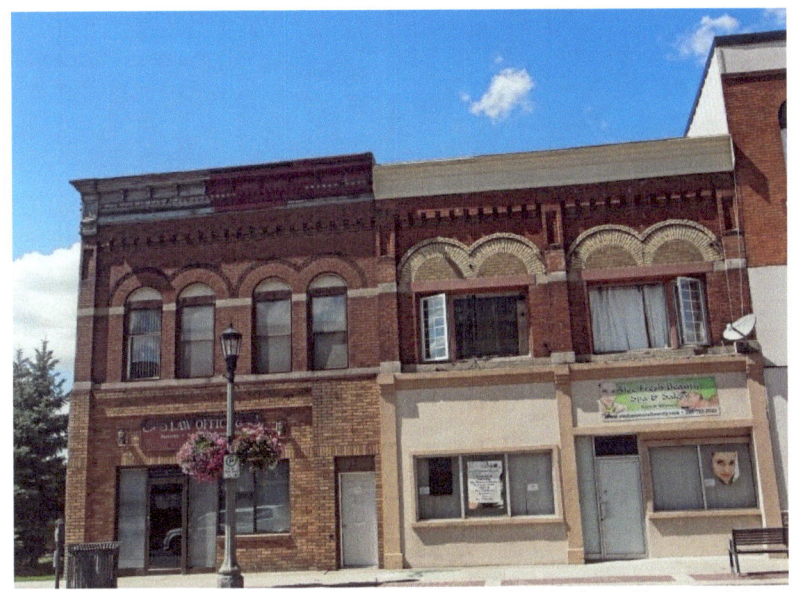

12 East Main Street – pilasters, bevelled dentil moulding, cornice brackets, Romanesque style window voussoirs, banding

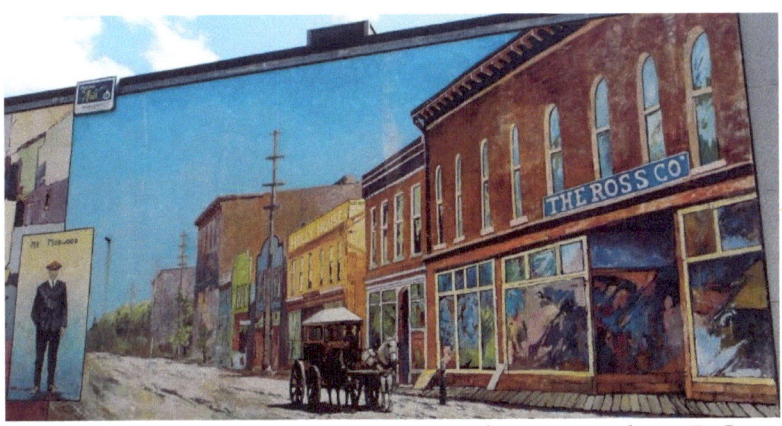

Main Street mural – 22 King Street – by Coquitlam B.C. artist Mike Svob - The Ross Company building and neighbouring stores

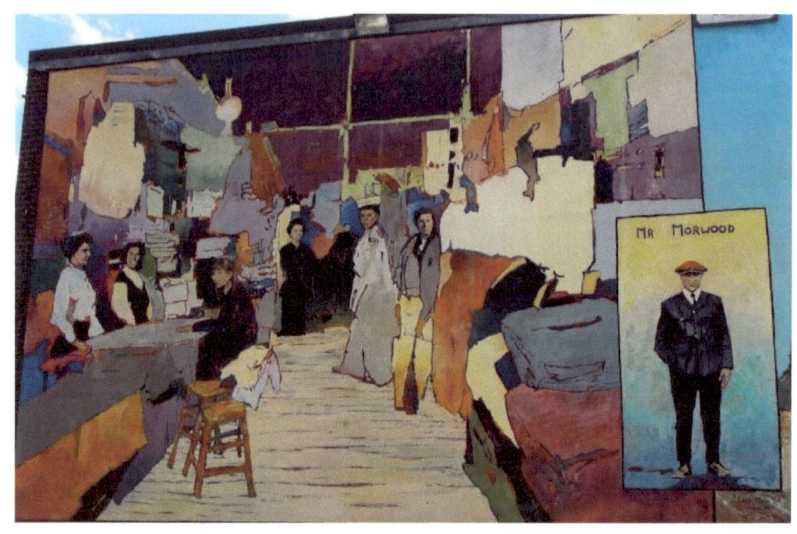

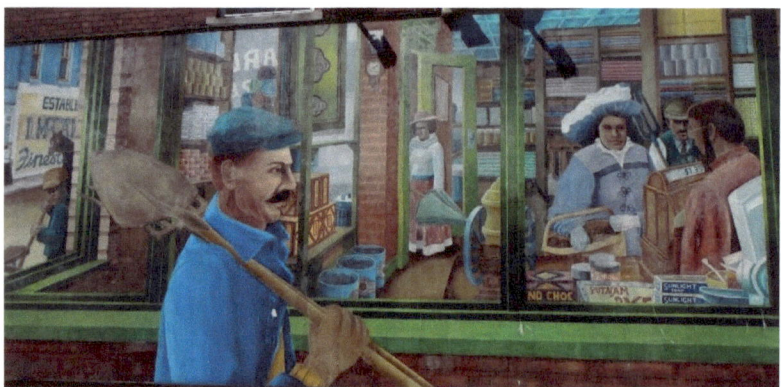

The inside of the Morwood Store, an original Welland retailer who opened for business in 1856 – you could buy anything from brass tacks to buck saws – a general store that boasted success for over 100 years

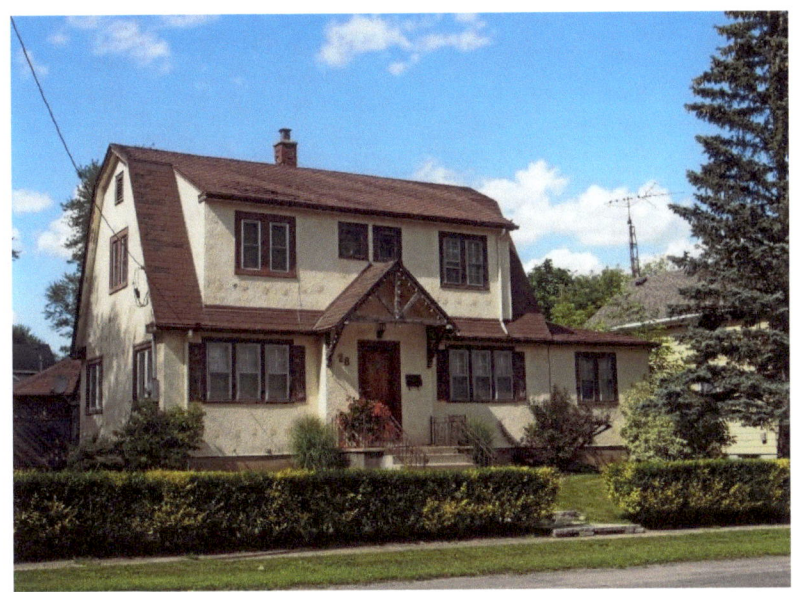

28 Elgin Street East – Neocolonial – gambrel roof, shed dormer

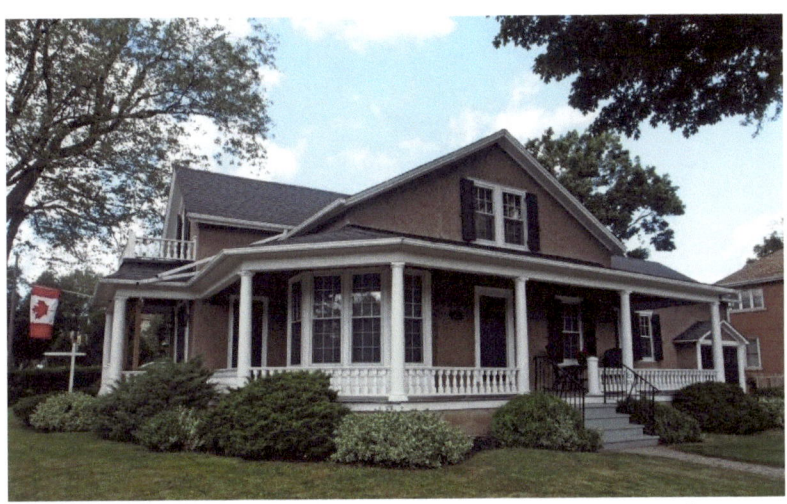

Elgin Street East – Twin Gates – 1855 – wraparound verandah

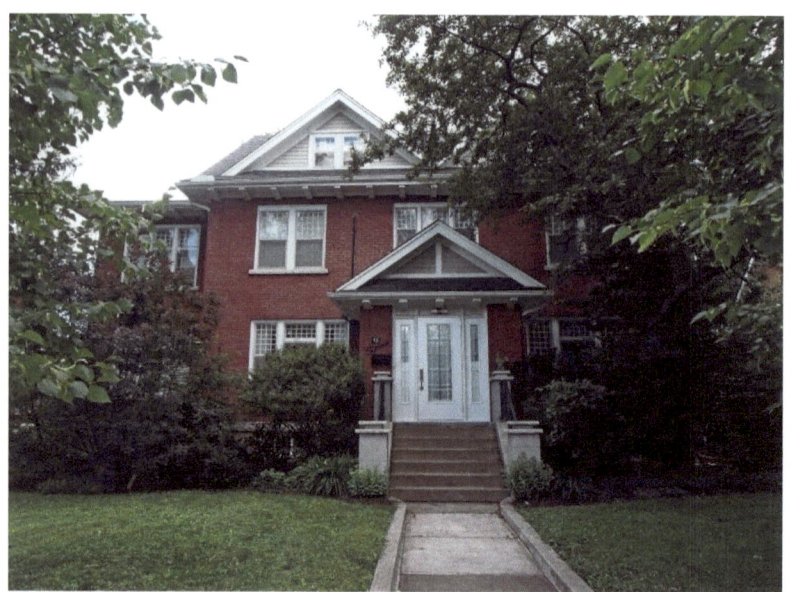

15 Elgin Street East – Italianate, pediment, sidelights

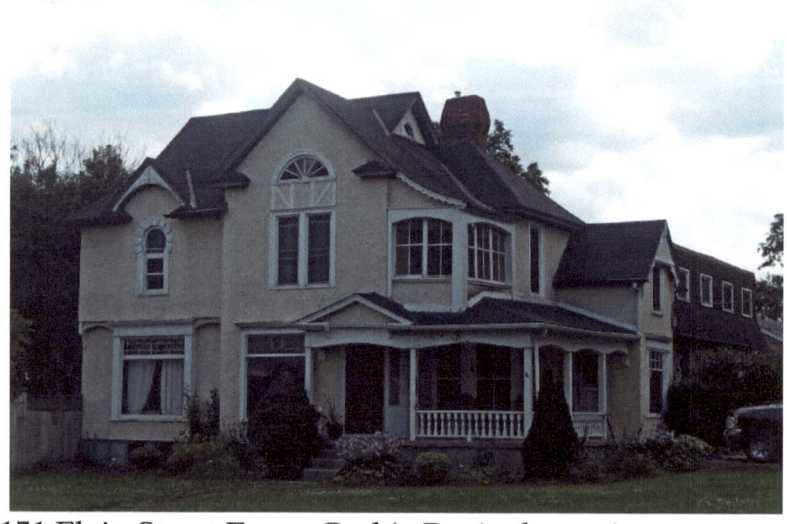

151 Elgin Street East – Gothic Revival, cornice return on gables, keyhole window, verge board trim

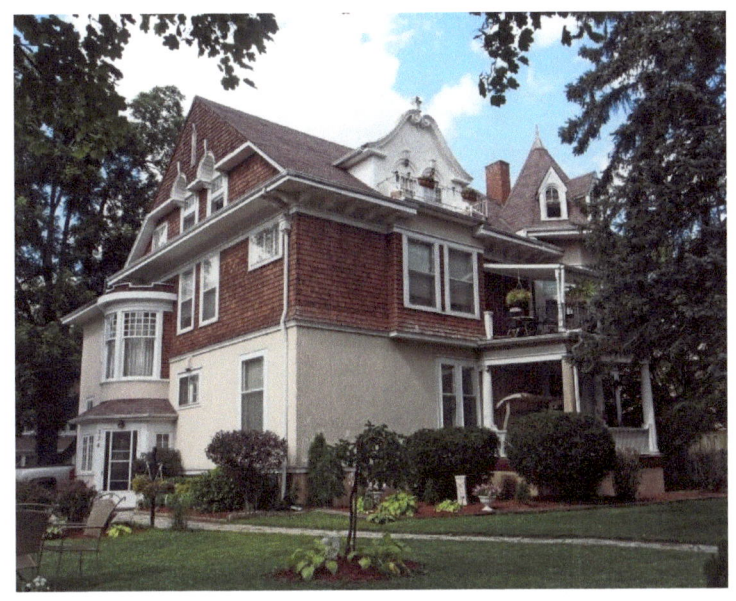

124 Elgin Street West – Queen Anne style, decorative dormer
with walkout balcony, two-storey bay window

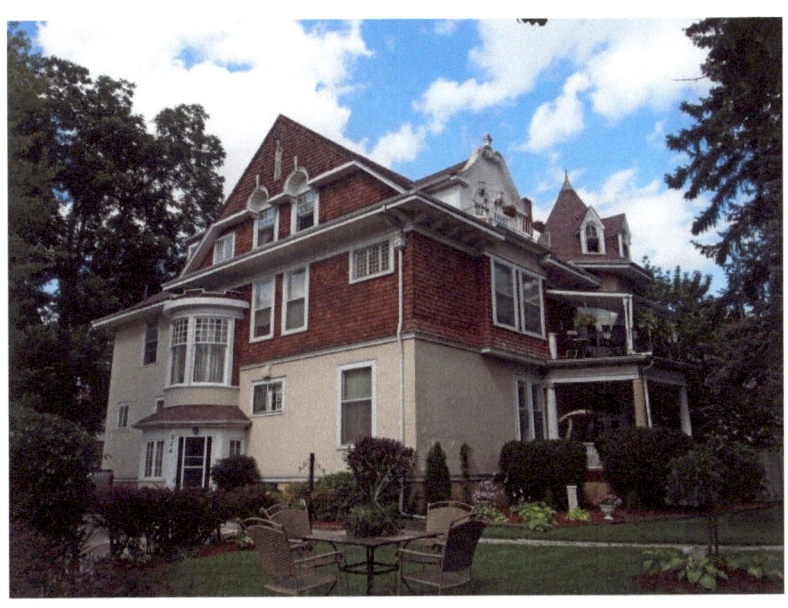

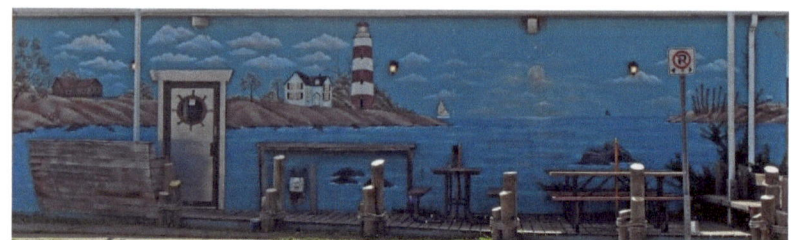
Mural

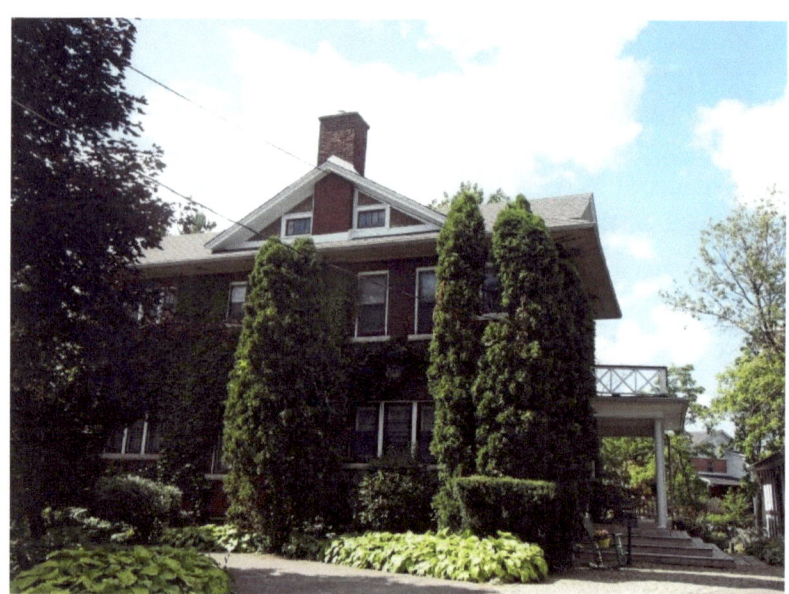
20 Evan Street

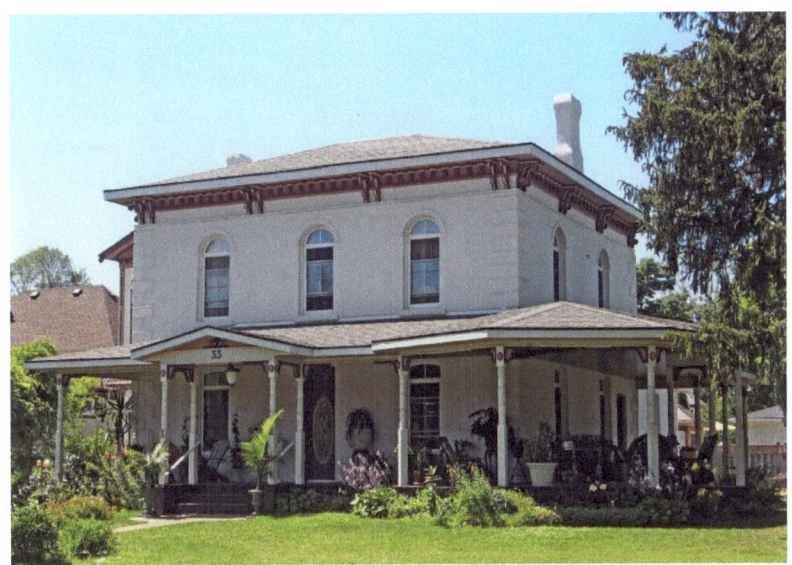

33 Frazer Street – Schooley House – 1870s – two storey Italianate "cube" design characterized by a square plan, hipped roof, cornice eave brackets and corner quoins; wraparound verandah

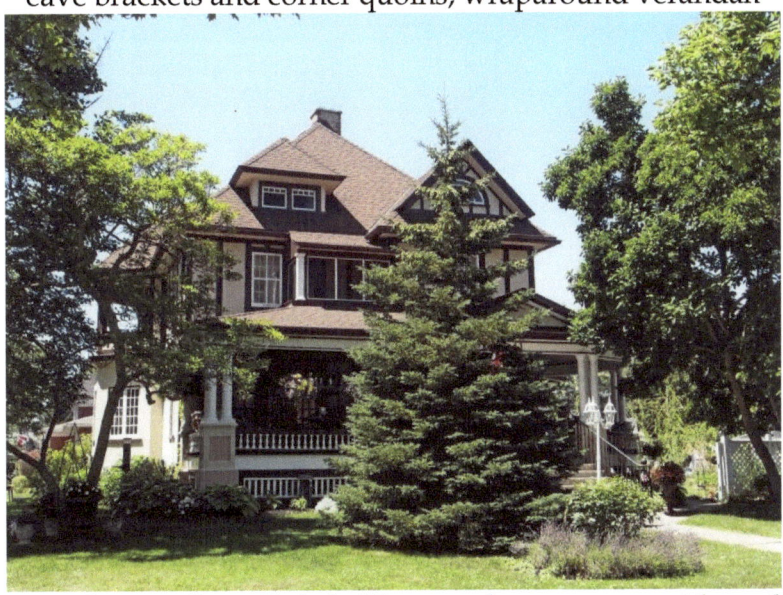

41 Frazer Street – Rose-Rohaly House – three-storey residence built c. 1906 – converted in 1920s to Tudor Revival style characterized by exposed timbers with stucco infill and multi-paned windows

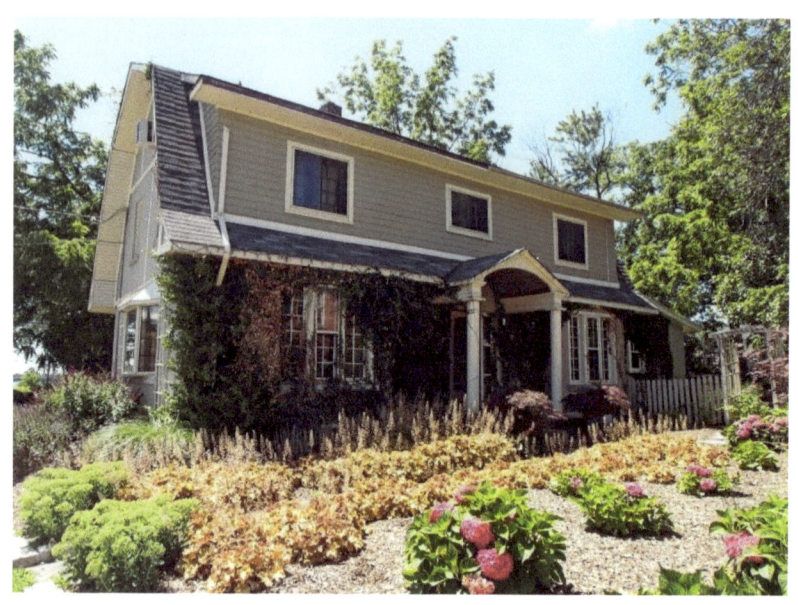

65 Frazer Street – Neocolonial, shed dormer

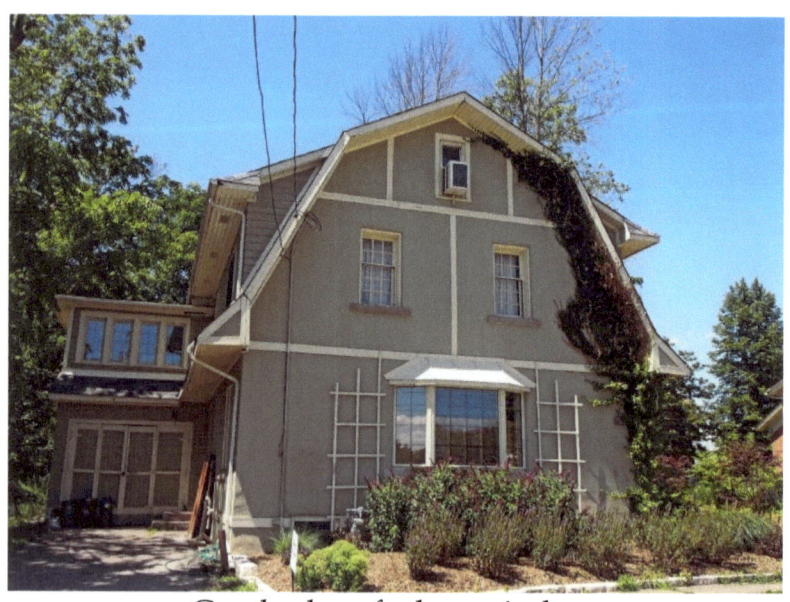

Gambrel roof – bay window

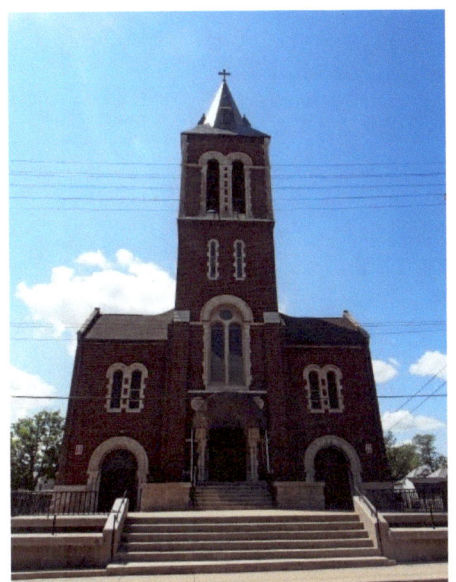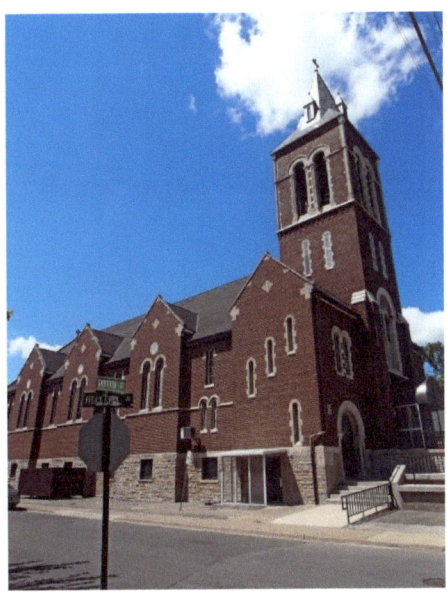

90 Griffith Street – St. Mary Roman Catholic Church – 1926
Romanesque style

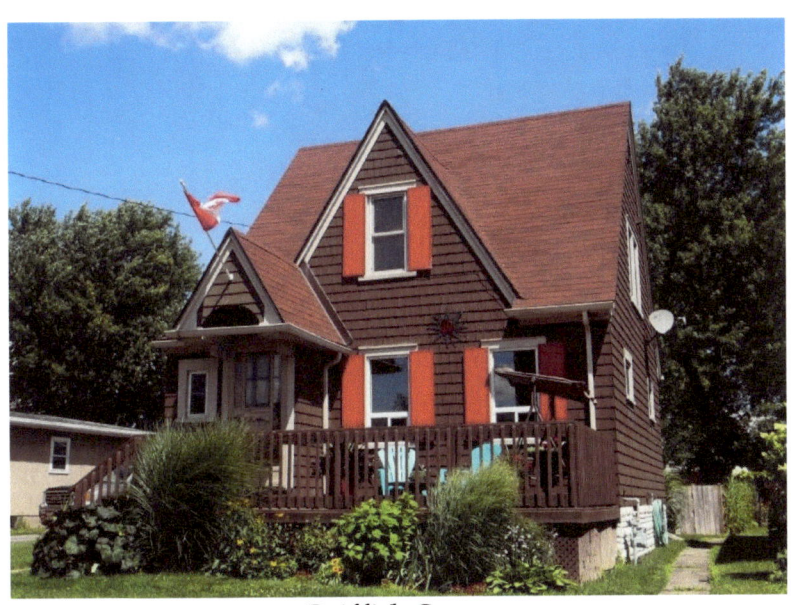

Griffith Street

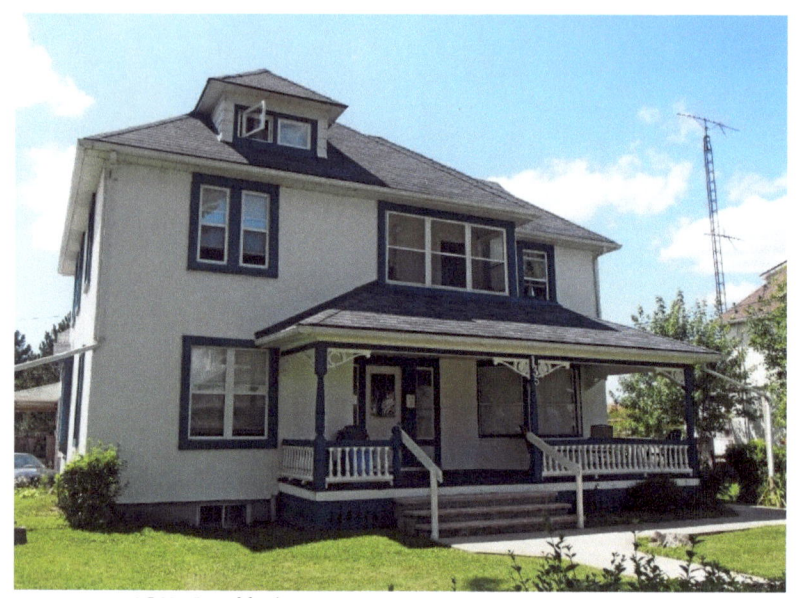

135 Griffith Street – Italianate, dormer

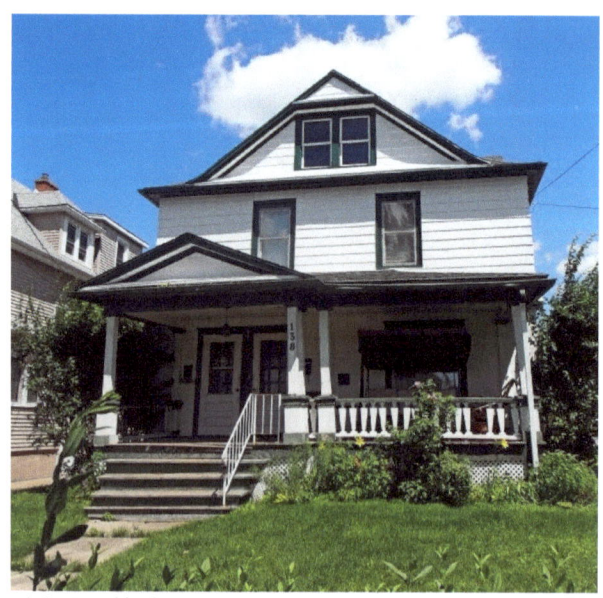

138 Griffith Street – Edwardian, pediment

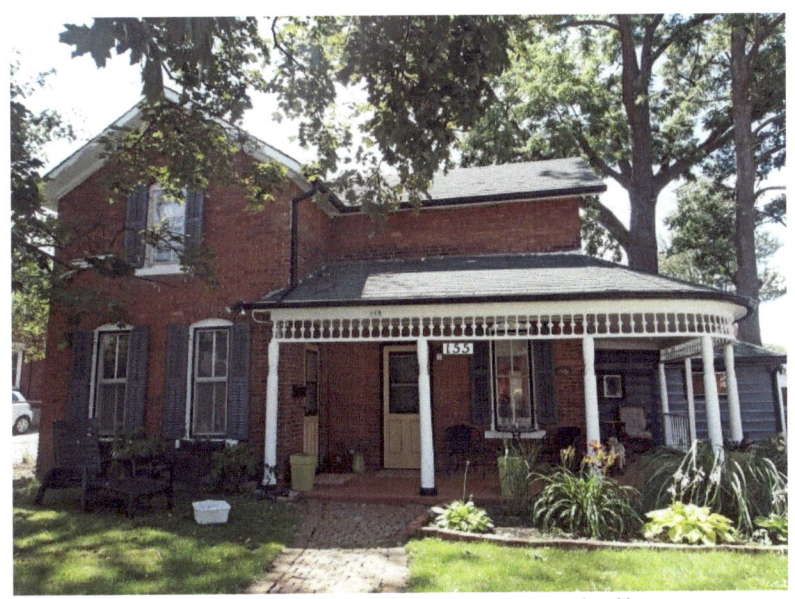

155 Hellems Avenue – 1884 - Gordon-Marshall two-storey, T-shaped brick home in the Italianate style, windows and doors display segmental arches capped with brick voussoirs, windows have their original two-over-two wavy panes of glass

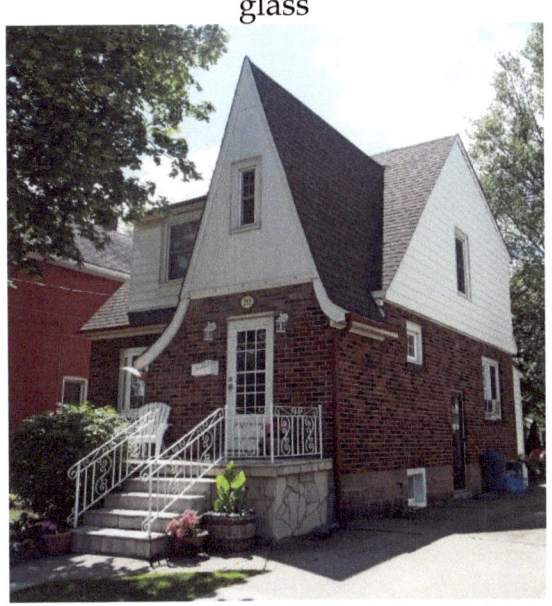

293 Hellems Avenue – vernacular

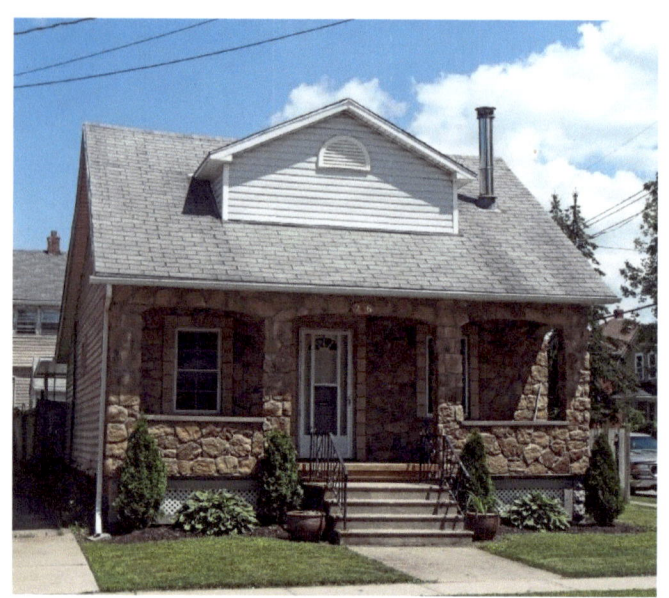

296 Hellems Avenue

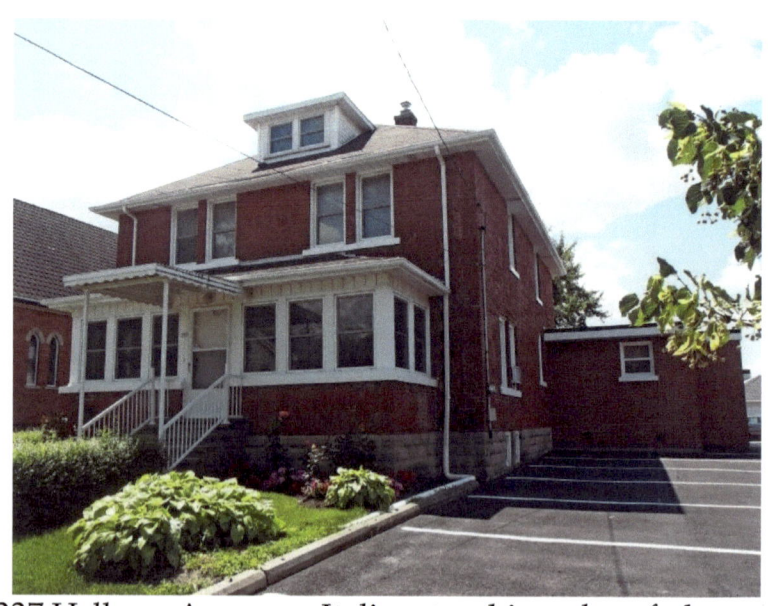

337 Hellems Avenue – Italianate – hipped roof, dormer

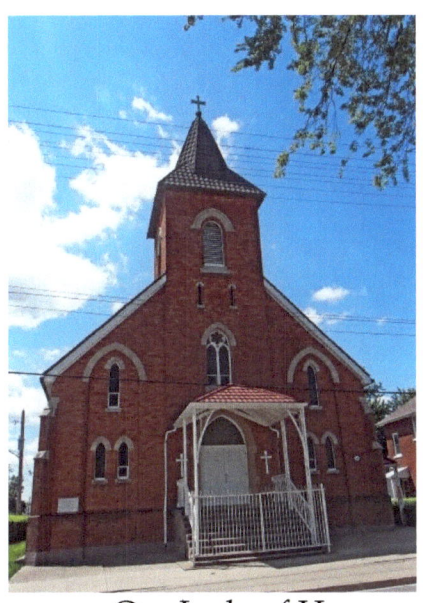

345 Hellems Avenue – Our Lady of Hungary Church – 1928
Lancet windows

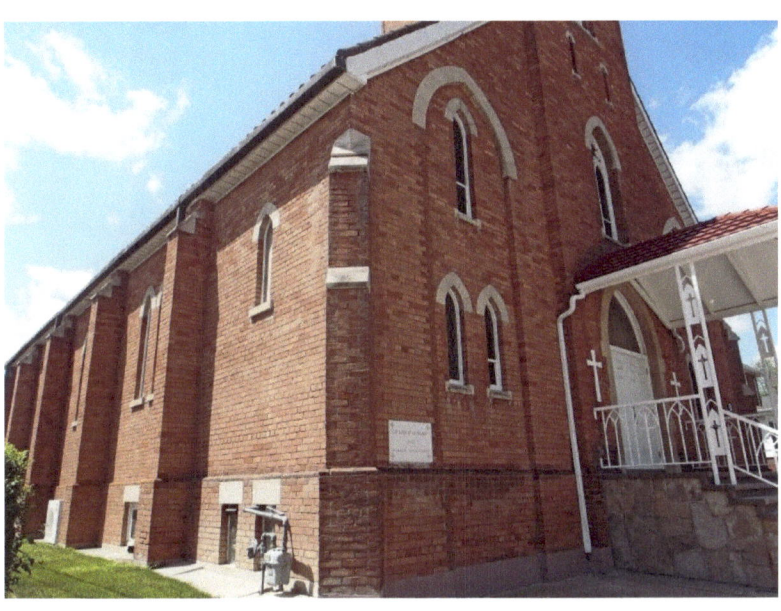

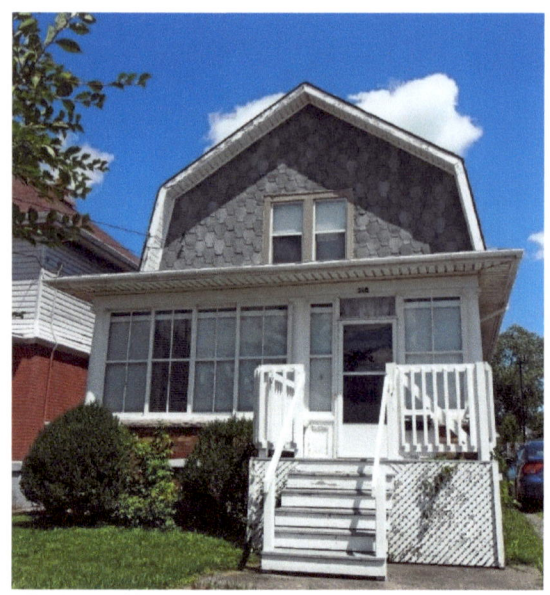

348 Hellems Avenue - gambrel roof

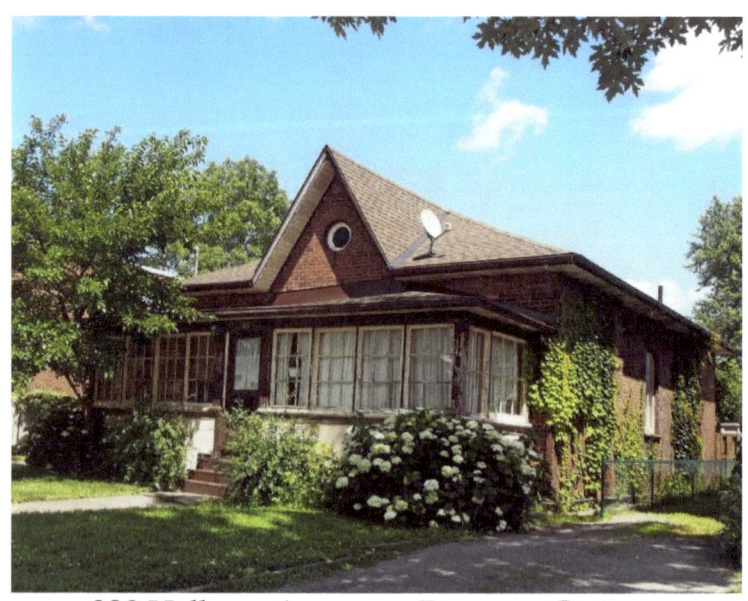

320 Hellems Avenue – Regency Cottage

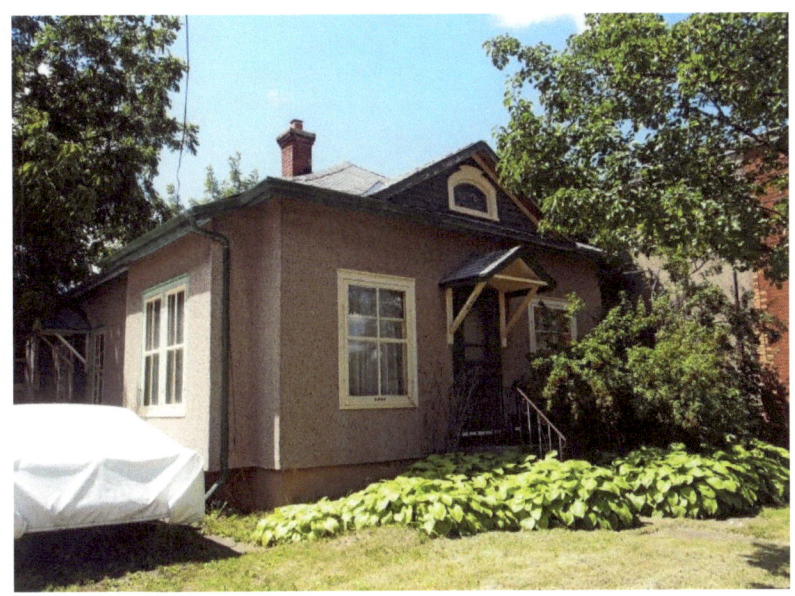

245 Hellems Avenue – Regency Cottage

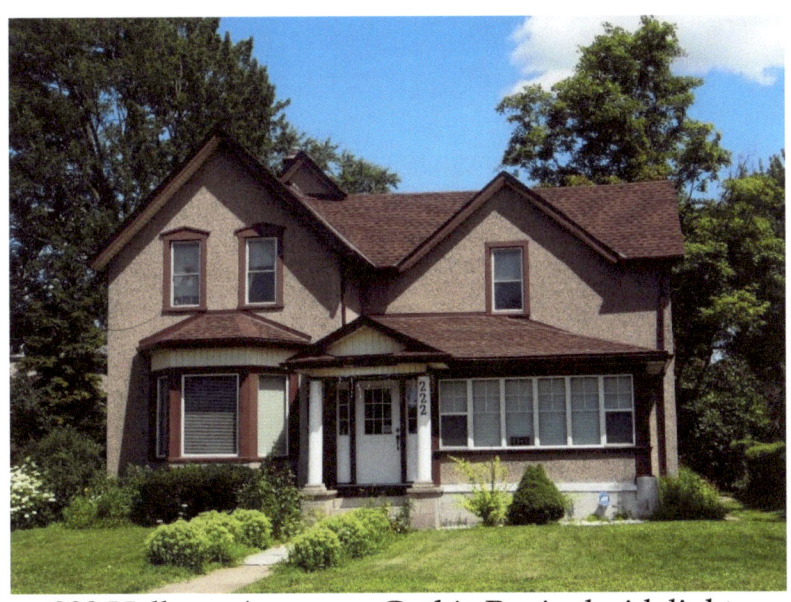

222 Hellems Avenue – Gothic Revival, sidelights

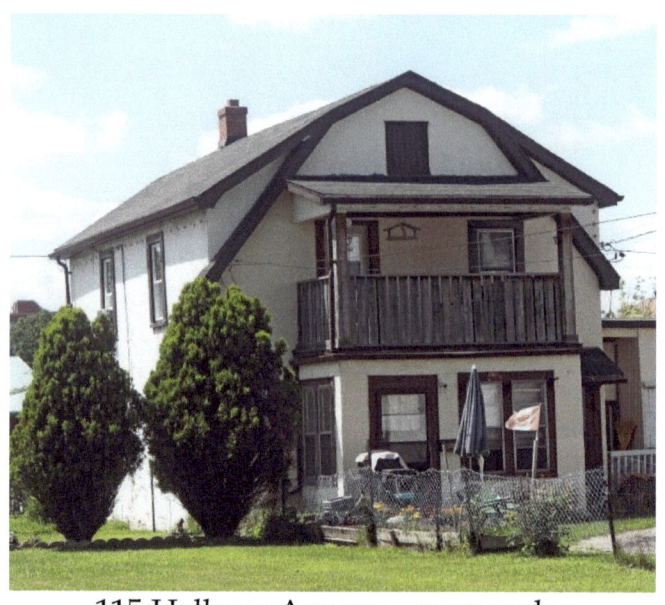

115 Hellems Avenue - vernacular

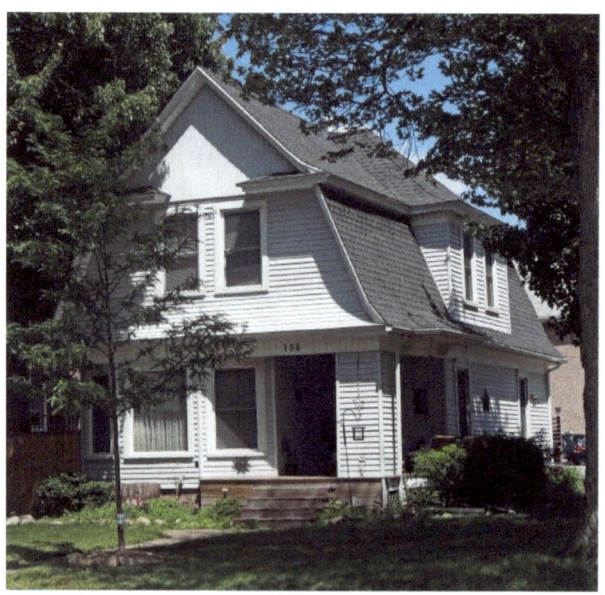

108 Hellems Avenue – vernacular - cornice return on gable, dormer

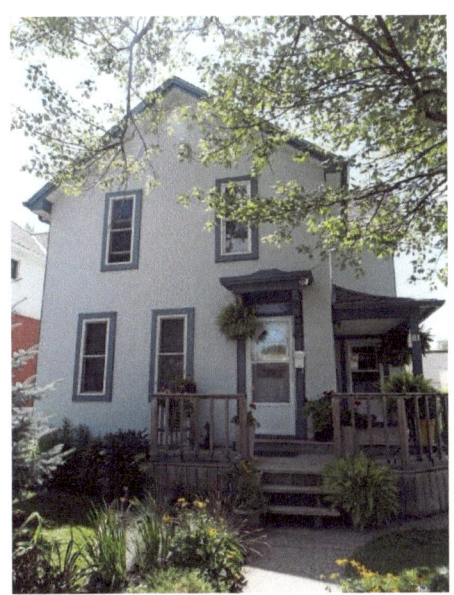

81 Hellems Avenue - Gothic

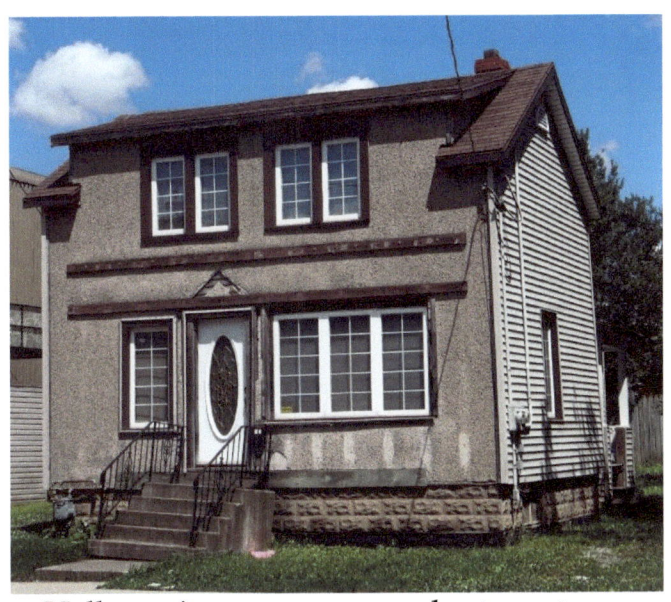

Hellems Avenue – vernacular two-storey

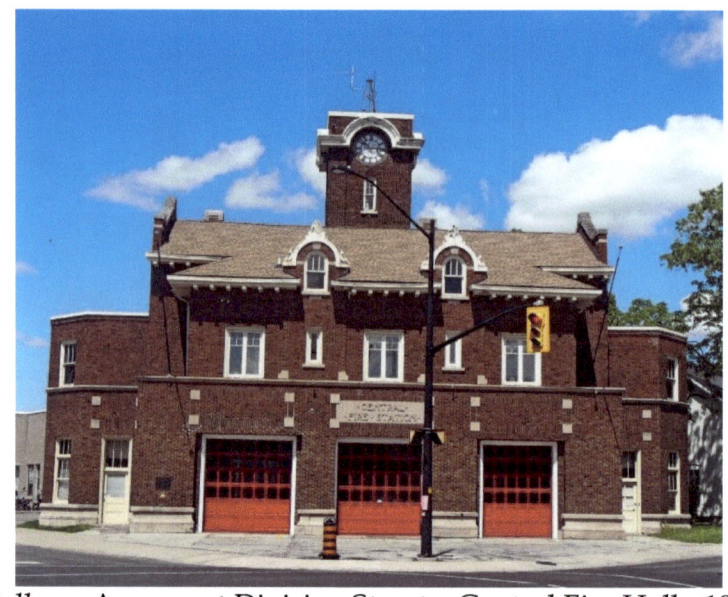

Hellems Avenue at Division Street – Central Fire Hall - 1920
Classical Revival details including the acroterions (Greek ornaments resembling fire helmets) above the semi-circular dormer windows

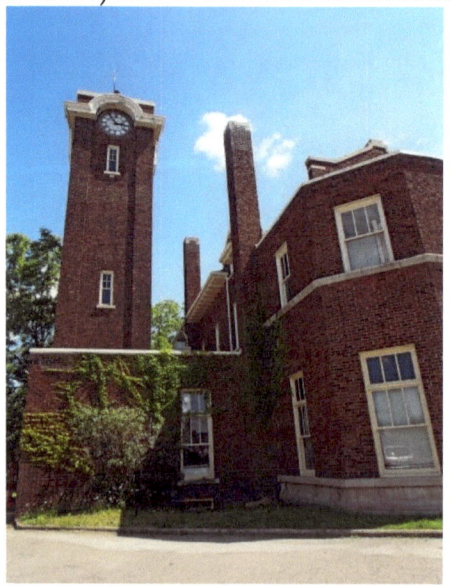

70-foot high, square, brick tower used to hang dry hoses has a four-faced clock

Architectural Terms

Banding: Different materials, colours or textures used in horizontal bands along a wall. Example: 12 East Main Street, Page 35	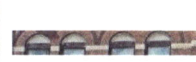
Bay Window: A window that projects out from a wall, in a semicircular, rectangular, or polygonal design. Used frequently in Gothic and Victorian designs. Example: 124 Elgin Street West, Page 39	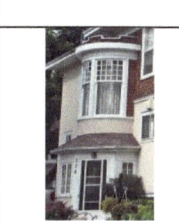
Brackets: a decorative or weight-bearing structural element which forms a right angle with one side against a wall and the other under a projecting surface such as an eave or roof. Example: 33 Frazer Street, Page 41	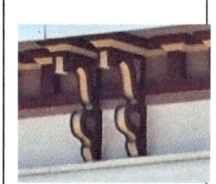
Buttress: a masonry structure built against or projecting from a wall which serves to support or reinforce the wall. In Canadian architecture, they are sometimes used for decoration. Example: 224 Division Street, Page 22	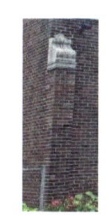
Capital: The uppermost finish or decoration on a column. An Ionic column has a small base, a thin elegant shaft, and a capital composed of volutes which are carved whirls or twists that take the form of a scroll. Example: 58 Burgar Street, Page 15	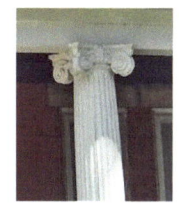

Cornice: originally the wooden overhang of the roof. With the use of stone, brick, iron and steel, the cornice is any projecting shelf at the top of a ceiling or roof. They can be very decorative. **Cornice Return:** decorative element on the end of a gable. Example: 165 Aqueduct Street, Page 7	
Cupola: A domed or curved roof rising from a building as a decorative element. Example: 224 Division Street, Page 22	
Dentil Moulding: an even series of rectangles used as ornamental decoration in cornices. Example: 12 East Main Street, Page 35	
Dormer: (French for "sleep") a gable end window that pierces through the plane of a sloping roof surface to create usable space in the top floor or attic of a building by adding headroom. Example: 152 Aqueduct Street, Page 6	
Gable: the triangular portion of a wall between the edges of a sloping roof. **Jacobean Gable:** the gable extends above the roofline. Example: 48 Burgar Street, Page 14	

Gambrel Roof: a symmetrical two-sided roof with two slopes on each side; the upper slope is positioned at a shallow angle, while the lower slope is steep. It is similar to a mansard roof, but a gambrel has vertical gable ends instead of being hipped at the four corners of the building. Example: 65 Bald Street, Page 12	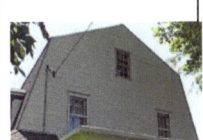
Hipped Roof: a roof where all sides slope downwards to the walls with no gables. Example: 33 Frazer Street, Page 41	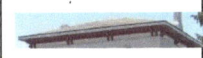
Keystones and Voussoirs: a voussoir is a wedge-shaped element used in building an arch. A keystone is the central stone that locks all the stones into position, allowing the arch to bear weight. A keystone is often enlarged and embellished. Example: 26 East Main Street, Page 34	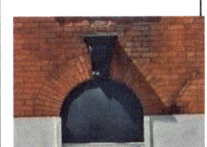
Lancet Window: a tall, narrow window with a pointed arch at its top.\n\nExample: 345 Hellems Avenue, Page 47	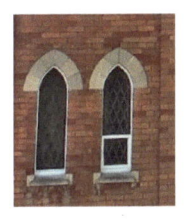
Oriel Window - These small areas were originally set into walls and galleries for the purpose of private prayer. Over time, any projecting window or area on an upper floor was called an oriel. Example: 166 Dennistoun Street, Page 18	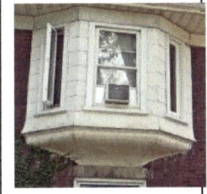

Palladian Window: a large window that is divided into three sections with the centre section larger than the two side sections and usually arched. Example: East Main Street, Page 30	
Pediment: a triangular section above the horizontal structure (entablature), typically supported by columns. The inside of the triangle is called the tympanum. Example: 233 Division Street, Page 20	
Pilaster: a slightly projecting column built into or applied to the face of a wall for additional structural support. Example: 12 East Main Street, Page 35	
Quoin: masonry blocks at the corner of a wall, often a decorative feature, usually larger or of a different colour than the rest of the wall. Example: 110 Bald Street, Page 9	
Sidelight: a window, usually with a vertical emphasis, that flanks a door, and is often used to emphasize the importance of a primary entrance. Example: 15 Elgin Street East, Page 38	

Turret: a small tower that projects from the wall of a building. Example: 30 Bald Street, Page 13	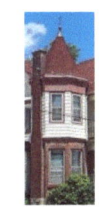
Verge board and Finial: also called bargeboards – hang from the projecting end of a roof and are often elaborately carved and ornamented. **Finial:** ornament added to the top of a gable, pinnacle, canopy or spire – a Gothic element. Example: 221 Division Street, Page 21	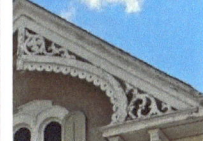
Window Hood: A **hood** is the piece found above window openings, usually of an ornate design, and covers the top third of the opening. Hoods are commonly placed above arched or curved openings on both windows and doors. Example: 102 East Main Street East, Page 31	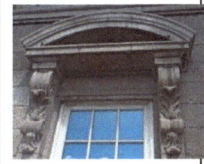

Classical Revival (1820 - 1860) – This style was an analytical, scientific, and dogmatic revival based on intensive studies of Greek and Roman buildings, concerned with the application of Greek plans and proportions to civic buildings. Schools, libraries, government offices, and most other civic buildings were built in the Classical Revival style. The white columned porches of the Classical Revival domestic buildings are identified with the mansions of wealthy land owners in Canada. Example: Hellems Avenue at Division Street, Page 52	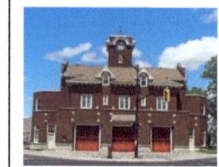
Edwardian, 1900-1930 – This style bridges the ornate and elaborate styles of the Victorian era and the simplified styles of the 20th century. Balanced facades, simple roof lines, dormer windows, large front porches, and smooth brick surfaces are its characteristics. Example: 110 Bald Street, Page 9	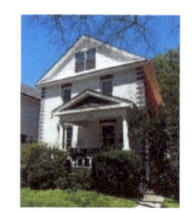
Gothic Revival, 1830-1890 – These decorative buildings have sharply-pitched gables with highly detailed verge boards, pointed-arch window openings, and dichromatic brickwork. It is a common style in Ontario. Example: 222 Hellems Avenue, Page 49	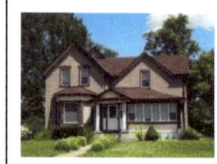
Italianate, 1850-1900 – It has wide-bracketed eaves, belvederes, wrap-around verandahs.

Example: 58 Burgar Street, Page 15 | 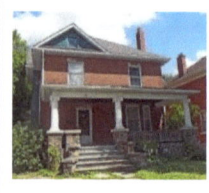 |

Neo-Classical (1810 - 1850) – This style was a direct result of the War of 1812. Many Upper Canadians returning from the war with the United States were second or third generation Loyalists who had inherited land and means from their forefathers. Once the conflict had passed, they had the money and the time to expand their holdings and indulge their architectural whims. Both residential and commercial buildings were constructed on the traditional Georgian plan, but they had a new gaiety and light-heartedness. Detailing became more refined, delicate, and elegant. Example: 102 East Main Street, Page 31	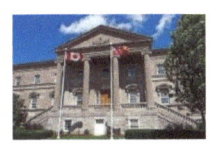
Neocolonial (also Colonial Revival, Georgian Revival or Neo-Georgian) architecture seeks to revive elements of architectural style of American colonial architecture of the period around the Revolutionary War which drew strongly from Georgian architecture of Great Britain. Architecture from the 18th and early 19th centuries in Ontario includes a wide assortment of detailing and ornament applied to a design centered around the fireplace and the source of water. Structures are typically two stories, have a symmetrical front facade with elaborate front doorways, often with decorative crown pediments, fanlights, and sidelights, symmetrical windows flanking the front entrance, often in pairs or threes, and columned porches. Example: 28 Elgin Street East, Page 37	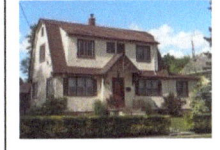

Queen Anne, 1885-1900 – This style is distinguished by an irregular outline featuring a combination of an offset tower, broad gables, projecting two-storey bays, verandahs, multi-sloped roofs, and tall, decorative chimneys. A mixture of brick and wood is common. Windows often have one large single-paned bottom sash and small panes in the upper sash. Example: 30 Bald Street, Page 13	
Regency Cottage, 1830-1860 – This style originated in England in 1815 and spread to Ontario later in the 19th century as British officers retired to Canada. It is a modest one-storey house with a low-pitched hip roof and has a symmetrical front façade. Example: 320 Hellems Avenue, Page 48	
Romanesque Revival, 1880-1910 – This style hearkens back to medieval architecture of the 11th and 12th centuries with a heavy appearance, blocky towers and rounded arches. Example: 25 Bald Street, Page 11	
Tudor Revival – exposed timbers with stucco infill, multi-paned windows. Example: 41 Frazer Street, Page 41	

Vernacular/Traditional Mode 1638 - 1950 Influenced but not defined by a particular style, vernacular buildings are made from easily available materials and exhibit local design characteristics. Example: 168 Dennistoun Street, Page 17	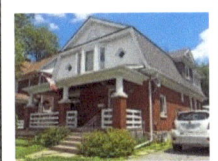
Victorian - In Ontario, a Victorian style building can be seen as any building built between 1840 and 1900 that doesn't fit into any of the other categories. It encompasses a large group of buildings constructed in brick, stone, and timber, using an eclectic mixture of Classical and Gothic motifs. Example: 131 Aqueduct Street, Page 8	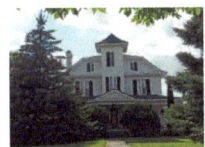

www.ingramcontent.com/pod-product-compliance
Lightning Source LLC
Chambersburg PA
CBHW040850180526
45159CB00001B/382